FRANCE

Message of Peace, Trust, Love and Faith

FRANCE

Message of Peace, Trust, Love and Faith

John Paul II

Compiled and Indexed
by the Daughters of St. Paul

ST. PAUL EDITIONS

Reprinted with permission from *L'Osservatore Romano,*
English Edition.

Library of Congress Cataloging in Publication Data

John Paul II, Pope, 1920-
    France—message of peace, trust, love, and faith.

    Includes index.
    1. Catholic Church—Sermons. 2. Sermons, English—
Translations from French. 3. Sermons, French—Translations
into English. I. Daughters of St. Paul.
II. Title.
BX1756.J64F7   252'.02   80-22231

ISBN 0-8198-2601-4 cloth
ISBN 0-8198-2602-2 paper

Photo Credits:

Felici—cover, 48, 69, 89, 175, 195,
213, color insert
Wide World Photos—17, 21, 26, 33,
63, 71, 81, 109, 115, 119, 135, 151,
169, 209, 221, 233

Printed in U.S.A. by the Daughters of St. Paul
50 St. Paul's Ave., Boston, MA 02130

The Daughters of St. Paul are an international congregation of
religious women serving the Church with the communications
media.

CONTENTS

FRANCE—ELDEST DAUGHTER OF THE CHURCH

On May 27, three days before his apostolic pilgrimage to France, the Holy Father sent the following message which was broadcasted by radio and television to the French people.

Three days before leaving for Paris, I wish to express in the first place my deep gratitude to all those who have invited me: UNESCO, the French Episcopate, the President and the civil authorities of France, and also to those who have manifested their expectations to me. For, in addition to the official authorities I have named, a large number of persons, from all walks of life, and in particular many young people, have expressed their sentiments, particularly their trust and their desire for this meeting, very often by letters. My thanks go to them! All that has been able to create a favorable climate which I feel already, and I would like to meet this expectation in the best way.

It happens that this journey in France takes place just a few weeks after the pastoral visit to Africa and within a month of a similar visit to Brazil. I trust that Providence and the light of the Holy Spirit will help me to carry out this pastoral journey, as a service imposed on me by my ministry as Successor of St. Peter, and also according to the spirit of St. Paul who went to strengthen the faith of the Churches, to receive their testimony and put them in communion with one another.

This journey attracts me for many reasons. It is an honor for me, but above all a duty, a responsibility.

In the first place, France is the eldest Daughter of the Church. And she has brought forth so many saints! I could add that there are many places on the soil of France to which I often go on pilgrimage in prayer and in my heart. Among them, only Lisieux has been able to find a place during this visit. But there are also Ars and many other places to which I am bound in spirit, and from where I have even received invitations.

How could I fail to recall, in this perspective, the cultural work of your country, its contribution to general culture and in the specifically Catholic field? How many famous names in your centuries-old tradition! Yes, in the very course of this century, how many figures whose influence has gone beyond your frontiers, and many of whom are personally very close to me. It is significant, moreover, that UNESCO, intended as an international organization to promote culture in all countries, should have established its headquarters in Paris.

Thus, when I think of the influence that French culture, in the fields of philosophy, history, and literature, and the thought of French theologians, have exercised and still exercise on so many men and societies, I cannot help thinking also of the special moment that the Church is living in this great country.

I well realize that the Church in France, French Catholicism, have found themselves in a special situation in the course of the last few years, since the Council. I do not propose to describe it here, or pass judgment on it. Everyone is well aware that it may be a question of what are called "growing pains." I hope that is a key to interpret this special situation which has been experienced in France since the Council.

I am quite convinced, in fact, that there are still in France, in the Church, in the nation and in society, immense forces, immense resources, which will permit her not only to continue to be herself, but also to put herself in the service of others.

Yes, the Church owes the people of France, which has received a great deal and also given a great deal, some of her finest pages: from the great religious orders, such as the Cistercians and the Carthusians, to the cathedrals, or to the missionary epic started in the last century. The generosity of her works and her thought has won her the friendship of a number of peoples, and among the poorest! May France continue to find there her *raison d'être!*

Over a year ago I was invited to Lourdes for the Eucharistic Congress, which will mark the centenary of these congresses, in July 1981. However, important converging circumstances, as I said, have induced me to anticipate this visit and arrive at Lourdes after first passing through Paris.

Having been invited, I in my turn invite the French people to this great meeting in prayer, in overall reflection, in a communion of spirits.

TO STRENGTHEN
THE FAITH OF
THE SONS OF FRANCE

On Friday afternoon, May 30, Pope John Paul left Rome to begin his apostolic pilgrimage in France. To the distinguished personalities, ecclesiastical and civil, who were present at the airport for his departure, the Holy Father delivered the following address.

1. About to leave once more Vatican City and the beloved soil of Italy, bound for France, I am happy to receive, Lord Cardinals, distinguished members of the Diplomatic Corps accredited to the Holy See, and representatives of the Italian Government, your cordial expression of affection and encouragement, which is, also, a testimony of interior participation in the intentions which inspire the purposes of today's apostolic pilgrimage.

For your presence, in which I see a happy auspice for the success of the commitment of the next few days, I wish to express to you my sincere and deep gratitude.

As Bishop of Rome and Successor of the Apostle Peter, there has been entrusted to me, by divine plan, the mission of being an instrument and sign of the unity of faith and communion among the various local Churches, confirming them in their adherence

I trust that Providence and the light of the Holy Spirit will help me to carry out this pastoral journey, as a service imposed on me by my ministry as Successor of St. Peter, and also according to the spirit of St. Paul who went to strengthen the faith of the Churches, to receive their testimony and put them in communion with one another.

This journey attracts me for many reasons. It is an honor for me, but above all a duty, a responsibility.

to Christ and to the Gospel. I have the privilege of carrying out this task mainly in Rome, the city of the spirit, where my brothers in the Episcopate often gather to meet the Vicar of Christ. However, modern possibilities of easy communication make it more and more natural that the Pope should come to and meet on the spot the bishops and the People of God.

2. France, a country of glorious tradition, is one of the great nations that have been marked by Christian faith from the dawn of their history and, after the fall of the Roman Empire, it was the first national community of the West to profess herself as a daughter of the Church: "Fille aînée de l'Eglise."

Throughout the course of the centuries, France offered a special contribution to the Catholic Church, through the enlightened and heroic witness of her saints, the vigorous doctrine of her teachers, and the apostolic courage of her missionaries. Today, too, she occupies a place of great importance in the universal Church, owing to her intelligent dynamism.

It is my intention to go to Lourdes in July of next year, on the occasion of the announced International Eucharistic Congress, but a pastoral visit to the heart of that nation seemed opportune, straightaway. It is this intention that inspires my stay in the capital, which sums up ideally in itself the values, the prospects and the anxieties of all Frenchmen. Furthermore, impelled by the same solicitude, I will also go to Lisieux, a blessed place, towards which Christianity and particularly the missions turn their admiring gaze, because of St. Thérèse, who with her message has put herself at the center, in the heart—according to her expression—of the Church, and of the missionary Church.

3. My visit has also another important goal: UNESCO. For some time I have been invited to meet the illustrious representatives of that organism, at their own headquarters, on the occasion of the 109th session of the Executive Council. I am happy to have this meeting, because true culture, which UNESCO has the institutional task of promoting all over the world, assumes outstanding importance for the development and defense of the dignity of man, who is not only the subject of instruction—in this field, too, the work that remains to be done is really considerable—but is called above all to mature to perfection the potentialities of his spiritual knowledge, in order to correspond to God's plans for the world and for history, in the framework of that peaceful progress in solidarity, for which we all hope.

So I leave the historic banks of the Tiber for the majestic ones of the Seine, and already this evening I shall find myself immersed in the poetic and solemn atmospere of Notre-Dame. I entrust to Mary, Lady of France and Châtelaine of Italy, the hope that my visit will strengthen the faith of the sons of that great country and give spirit to their courage of testimony. With these thoughts, I leave you my cordial greetings, good wishes and blessing.

CATHOLICS OF FRANCE, BE PROUD OF YOUR FAITH!

On arrival at Orly Airport on May 30, John Paul II was welcomed by Cardinals Francois Marty, Archbishop of Paris; Roger Etchegaray, Archbishop of Marseilles and President of the French Episcopal Conference; by the Apostolic Nuncio, Archbishop Angelo Felici; and by the Prime Minister of France, Mr. Raymond Barre.

The Holy Father and his suite then boarded a helicopter which took them to Place Georges Clemenceau in the center of Paris where they were welcomed by President Valery Giscard d'Estaing and his wife. The Pope, accompanied by the President, travelled in an open car to the Place de la Concorde. On arrival there, His Holiness was officially welcomed to France in a speech by President Giscard d'Estaing. In reply John Paul II delivered the following address.

Mr. President,

I am particularly touched by the words you have just addressed to me, at my arrival on the soil of France. I thank you warmly for them. You have done so on your personal behalf, you have done so on behalf of the French people, to whom, in your person, I would like to address my first message.

1. Praised be Jesus Christ! Yes, it was precisely thus, with these words filled with fervor and thanksgiving, that I wished, on the evening of my election as Bishop of Rome and universal Pastor, to

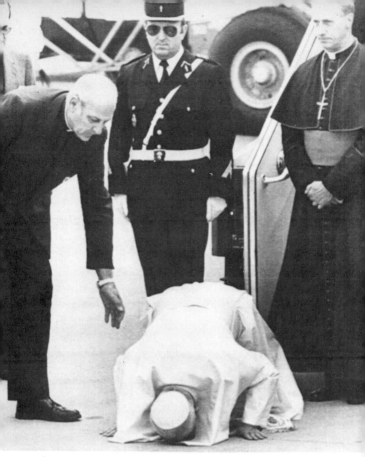

Praised be Jesus Christ!... It was precisely with these words, filled with fervor and thanksgiving, that I wished...to inaugurate my ministry of preaching the Gospel.

Now I have just brought this same greeting to France, with all my heart, with all my affection, saying to her: I am deeply happy to visit you in these days, and to show you my desire to serve you in each of your children. The message that I wish to deliver to you is a message of peace, trust, love and faith.

inaugurate my ministry of preaching the Gospel. I took this greeting in the first place to my diocesans on the banks of the Tiber, who had just been entrusted to me to guide them according to the plans of divine Providence. I took it afterwards to other peoples, to other local Churches, with all the content of esteem, pastoral solicitude and also of hope with which it is charged.

Now I have just brought this same greeting to France, with all my heart, with all my affection, saying to her: I am deeply happy to visit you in these days, and to show you my desire to serve you in each of your children. The message that I wish to deliver to you is a message of peace, trust, love and faith. Of faith in God, of course, but also, if I may express myself in this way, of faith in man, of faith in the marvelous possibilities that have been given to him, in order that he may use them wisely and for the sake of the common good, for the glory of the Creator.

To all the sons and daughters of this great nation, to all, the Pope offers his most cordial wishes, in the name of the Lord. France symbolizes for the world a country with a very ancient and full history. A country with an incomparable artistic and cultural heritage, the influence of which is no longer to be described. How many peoples have benefited from the French genius, which marked their own roots, and is still for them a source of pride and also at the same time, it may be said, a kind of reference! The role of France continues in the international community, at the level which is hers, but with a spirit of openness and a concern to make a contribution both to the main international problems and to the situations of the less favored regions. In the course of my preceding journeys, I was able to observe the place she holds beneath other skies. But more than to the fullness of the means used, which are necessarily limited, she owes her place to her people, to the men and women, the heirs to her civilization.

2. It is these men and women, the soul of France, that I will meet in these days. How could I fail to be touched by the welcome you bid me here, in your capital? Many of you have written to me before this visit, and this evening you are here in large numbers to welcome me. Unfortunately I cannot thank each one individually or shake all the hands that you would like to stretch out to me. But before you, to the representatives of the national sovereignty, I would like to bear witness to my deep gratitude.

Mr. President, you whom your fellow countrymen have designated to assume the highest responsibility in the State, deign, therefore, to accept the grateful homage that I address to the whole French people. I shall add sentiments of satisfaction for the extreme availability that Your Excellency, and also Mr. Prime Minister and the government, displayed as soon as my plan became known to them.

You at once understood the specific nature of this journey: a pastoral journey, above all, to visit and encourage Catholics in France; a journey which also intends to express my esteem and friendship for the whole population, and I am thinking here in particular of the members of other Christian confessions, of the Jewish community and of the Islamic religion. My desire was that this journey might be carried out in simplicity and dignity, arranging also, whenever possible, contacts and meetings. You gave all your collaboration to the implementation of the program, and I appreciate it all the more in that meticulous preparation was necessary. I think, finally, of the persons for whom these events cause extra work. All that is part of hospitality, a virtue on which France can rightly pride herself. Really, I express my heartfelt thanks to everyone.

3. I greet you very specially, dear Catholics of France, my brothers and sisters in Christ, my friends. You have invited me to see, fifteen hundred years or almost so after the baptism of your nation, that faith is still alive here, young and dynamic, that there is no lack of generosity in your country. It is even expressed by a seething of initiatives, researches, reflections. You must, in fact, cope with problems that are often new, or at least with new problematics. The context in which you live is evolving rapidly, according to cultural and social changes which are not without gradually influencing morals and mentalities. A multitude of questions arises before you. What is to be done? How to meet the fundamental needs of modern man, which reveal finally an immense need of God?

In union with your bishops, and in particular with the dear Cardinal Archbishop of Paris and the President of the French Episcopal Conference, I have come to encourage you in the way of the Gospel, a narrow way, certainly, but the royal, sure way tested by generations of Christians, taught by the saints and the blesseds on whom your country prides itself, the way along which, just like you, your brothers in the universal Church endeavor to walk. This way does not pass through resignation, renunciation or abandonment. It does not resign itself to the dulling of the moral sense, and it would like the civil law itself to elevate man. It does not try to bury itself, to remain unnoticed, but on the contrary it requires the joyful boldness of the Apostles. So it banishes faint-heartedness, while being perfectly respectful with regard to those who do not share the same ideal. If the Church claims religious freedom for herself, in fact, and if she has multiple reasons for expressing satisfaction at enjoying it in France, it is natural that she should also respect the convictions of others. She asks, on her part, that she should be permitted to live, to bear witness publicly, and to appeal to consciences.

"Recognize your dignity, O Christian," the great Pope St. Leo said. And I, his unworthy Successor, I say to you, my Catholic brothers and sisters in France: Recognize your dignity! Be proud of your faith, of the gift of the Spirit that the Father has bestowed on you! I come among you as a poor man, with the unique riches of the faith, a pilgrim of the Gospel. Give the Church and the world the example of your unfailing faithfulness and your missionary zeal. My visit to your country is intended, not only as a testimony of solidarity with regard to your pastors, but also as an appeal for a new outburst of enthusiasm in face of the numerous tasks that are offered to you.

I feel that, in the depths of your hearts, you will hearken to this exhortation. I address it, on my arrival on the soil of France, to all those who are listening to me, and I shall then have the opportunity to take it up again these days, talking with the bishops, the priests, the men and women religious, the laity engaged in the apostolate, meeting the workers and the young, men of thought and of science. A very special moment will be reserved for UNESCO, which has its seat in your capital. It seemed to me very important, indeed, to respond to its kind invitation, in order to greet an exceptional Areopagus of witnesses to the culture of our time, and to convey the Church's own testimony.

This first contact must now be concluded. I am going to the Basilica of Notre-Dame, the Mother of the churches of this diocese, and one of the most venerable religious buildings of this nation. There I wish to entrust to the Lord and to the Blessed Virgin my wishes for the whole of the French people. God bless France!

LIFE'S MEANING
IN THE ANSWER
TO GOD'S QUESTION:
"DO YOU LOVE ME?"

*After the official welcome by the President of France, the Holy
Father, accompanied by Cardinal Marty of Paris, drove in
an open car to Notre-Dame. At an altar erected outside the
cathedral, he concelebrated Mass with some French Cardinals,
and also with Cardinals Casaroli and Macharski (of Krakow).
After the reading of the Gospel His Holiness preached the following homily.*

1. *Do you love?*

A fundamental question, a common question. It is
the question that opens the heart—and that gives its
meaning to life. It is the question that decides man's
true dimension. In it, it is the whole man who must
express himself, and who must also, in it, transcend
himself.

Do you love me?

This question was asked, a moment ago, in this
place. It is a historic place, a sacred place. Here, we
meet the genius of France, the genius that expressed
itself in the architecture of this temple eight centuries
ago and that is always there, to bear witness to man.
Man, indeed, through all the formulas with which he
tries to define himself, cannot forget that he, too, is
a temple: he is the temple in which the Holy Spirit

dwells. For this reason, man raised this temple which has borne witness to him for eight centuries: Notre-Dame.

Here, in this place, in the course of our first meeting, this question had to be asked: "Do you love me?" But it must be asked everywhere and always. This question is put to man by God. And man must continually ask himself this question.

THIS TRIPLE QUESTION

2. This question was put to Peter by Christ. Christ asked it three times, and three times Peter answered. "Simon, son of John, do you love me?—Yes, Lord, you know that I love you" (Jn. 21:15-17).

Peter committed himself already, with this question and with this answer, along the way that was to be his until the end of his life. He was to be followed everywhere by the admirable dialogue in which he had also heard three times: "Be the shepherd of my sheep.... Be the shepherd of my lambs.... Be the shepherd of this fold of which I am the door and the Good Shepherd" (cf. Jn. 10:7).

Forever, to the end of his life, Peter was to advance along the way, accompanied by this triple question: "Do you love me?" And he measured all his activities by the answer he had given then. When he was called before the Sanhedrin. When he was put in prison in Jerusalem, a prison from which he should not have come out...and from which, nevertheless, he came out. And when he left Jerusalem towards the north, to Antioch, and then, even further, from Antioch to Rome. And when in Rome he had persevered to the end of his days, he experienced the power of the words according to which another was to lead him where he did not wish to go... (cf. Jn. 21:18).

He knew too that, thanks to the power of these words, the Church was assiduously devoted "to the apostles' teaching and fellowship, to the breaking of bread and the prayers"...and that "the Lord added to their number day by day those who were being saved" (Acts 2:42-48).

It was so in Jerusalem. Then in Antioch. Then in Rome. And then again here, in the west and north of the Alps: in Marseilles, Lyons and Paris.

LAND OF SAINTS

3. Peter can never detach himself from this question: "Do you love me?" He takes it with him wherever he goes. He takes it through the centuries, through the generations. In the midst of new peoples and new nations. In the midst of ever new languages and races. He alone takes it, and yet he is no longer alone. Others take it with him. Paul, John, James, Andrew, Irenaeus of Lyons, Benedict of Norcia, Martin of Tours, Bernard of Clairvaux, the "Poor Man" of Assisi, Joan of Arc, Francis of Sales, Jane Frances de Chantal, Vincent de Paul, John Mary Vianney, Thérèse of Lisieux.

On this land which I have the privilege of visiting today, here, in this city, there have been, and there are, many men and women who have known and who still know today that their whole life has a value and meaning solely and exclusively to the extent to which it is an answer to this same question: Do you love me? Do you love me? They have given, and give, their answer in a complete and perfect way—a heroic answer—or else in a common, ordinary way. But in any case they know that their lives, that human life in general, has a value and a meaning to the extent to which it is the answer to this question: Do you love? It is only thanks to this question that life is worth living.

I come here in their footsteps. I visit their earthly country. I commend to their intercession France and Paris, the Church and the world. The answer they have given to this question: "Do you love?" has a universal significance, an abiding value. It constructs in the history of mankind the world of good. Only love constructs this world. It constructs it with difficulty. It must struggle to give it shape: it must struggle against the forces of evil, sin, hatred, against the lust of the flesh, against the lust of the eyes and against the pride of life (cf. 1 Jn. 2:16).

This struggle is an incessant one. It is as old as the history of man. In our time, this struggle to give shape to our world seems to be greater than ever. More than once we wonder, trembling, if hatred will not get the better of love, war of peace, destruction of construction.

How extraordinary the eloquence of this question of Christ's is: "Do you love?"! It is fundamental for one and all of us. It is fundamental for the individual and for society, for the nation and for the state. It is fundamental for Paris and for France: "Do you love?"

PETER'S FAITH

4. Christ is the cornerstone of this construction. He is the cornerstone of this shape that the world, our human world, can take thanks to love.

Peter knew this, he whom Christ asked three times: "Do you love me?" Peter knew, he who, when put to the test, denied his Master three times. His voice trembled when he answered: "Yes, Lord; you know that I love you" (Jn. 21:15). However, he did not answer: "And yet, Lord, I disappointed you"— but: "Lord, you know that I love you." Saying that, he knew already that Christ is the cornerstone, on which, in spite of all human weakness, this construction that will have the form of love can grow in him, Peter. Through all situations and through all trials. To the end. That is why he will write one day, in his letter that we have just read, the text on Jesus Christ, the cornerstone on which "like living stones be yourselves built into a spiritual house, to be a holy priesthood, to offer spiritual sacrifices acceptable to God through Jesus Christ..." (1 Pt. 2:5).

All that means nothing else than to answer, always and constantly, with tenacity and consistency, this one question: Do you love? Do you love me? Do you love me more?

It is, in fact, this answer, namely, this love, which makes us "a chosen race, a royal priesthood, God's own people..." (1 Pt. 2:9).

It is this that makes us proclaim the wonderful deeds of Him who "called (us) out of darkness into his marvelous light" (ibid.).

Peter knew all that in the absolute certainty of his faith. And he knows all that, and continues to profess it also in his successors. He knows, yes, and he confesses that this cornerstone, which gives the whole construction of human history the shape of love, justice and peace, was, is and will be, really, the stone rejected by men..., by men, by many of those who are the builders of the destiny of the world; and yet, in spite of that, it is really He, Jesus Christ, who was, who is and who will be the cornerstone of human history. It is from Him that, in spite of all conflicts, objections and denials, in spite of the darkness and the clouds that continue to gather on the horizon of history—and you know how threatening they are today, in our age!—it is from Him that the abiding construction will spring up, it is on Him that it will rise, and it is through Him that it will develop. Only love has the power to do that. Only love does not know decline.

Only love lasts forever (cf. 1 Cor. 13:8). Alone, it constructs the shape of eternity in the earthly and short-lived dimensions of the history of man on the earth.

A SACRED PLACE

5. We are here in a sacred place: Notre-Dame. This splendid construction, a treasure of Gothic art, was dedicated by your ancestors to the Mother of God. They dedicated it to her who, among all human beings, gave the most perfect answer to this question: Do you love? Do you love me? Do you love me more?

Her whole life was, in fact, a perfect answer, without any error, to this question.

It was opportune, therefore, that I should begin in a place dedicated to Mary my meeting with Paris and with France, a meeting to which I was so kindly invited by the authorities of the state and the city, by the Church and her pastors. My visit on Monday to the headquarters of UNESCO in Paris takes on thereby its complete frame of reference and the dimension in keeping with my mission of witness and apostolic service.

This invitation is a very precious one for me. I highly appreciate it. I also wish, according to my

It is from Christ that, in spite of all conflicts, objections and denials, in spite of the darkness and the clouds that continue to gather on the horizon of history—and you know how threatening they are today, in our age!—it is from Him that the abiding construction will spring up, it is on Him that it will rise, and it is through Him that it will develop. Only love has the power to do that. Only love does not know decline.

Only love lasts forever (cf. 1 Cor. 13:8). Alone, it constructs the shape of eternity in the earthly and short-lived dimensions of the history of man on the earth.

possibilities and according to the grace given to me by my office, to respond to this invitation and make it achieve its purpose.

That is why I rejoice that our first meeting takes place in the presence of the Mother of God, before her who is our hope. I wish to entrust to her the service that falls to me to carry out among you. It is she, too, whom I ask, together with you all, dear brothers and sisters, that this service may be useful and fruitful for the Church in France, for man and for the modern world.

MAN'S FUTURE

6. There are many places in your country where my thought and my heart very often go, maybe every day, on pilgrimage: the shrine of the Immaculate Virgin in Lourdes, Lisieux, and Ars, where I shall not be able to go this time, and Annecy, where I have long been invited without having been able, so far, to fulfill my desire.

Before my eyes is France, Mother of saints throughout so many generations and centuries. Oh, how much I wish they would all return in our century, and in our generation, in proportion to its needs and its responsibilities!

At this first meeting, I hope that one and all will hear in all its eloquence the question that Christ put formerly to Peter: Do you love? Do you love me? May this question resound and find a deep echo in each of us!

The future of man and of the world depends on it: shall we listen to this question? Shall we understand its importance? How shall we answer it?

TO THE PEOPLE UNABLE TO ATTEND

On re-entering the Cathedral after the Mass outside Notre-Dame on Friday evening, May 30, the Holy Father broadcasted the following message over French radio to those unable to attend the Mass.

This evening, after having celebrated Mass in the heart of the French capital in front of Notre-Dame, I am thinking of all those who would have liked to take part in this gathering around the Pope or in the celebrations that will follow, but who have had to stay at home: of the sick, of all those who are confined to bed in hospitals, to whom I wish solace and peace; of the handicapped and their families; of prisoners, whom I visit in spirit and to whom I wish faith in God's mercy, hope and the faithful support of their families; to workers, whose hours of work or spell of public duty make it difficult for them to join in these manifestations; finally, of all those who, for other reasons, will not be able to satisfy their desire to see or hear the Pope. I tell you all, dear friends, of my esteem. I assure you of my prayer and my cordial wishes for your families.

And as I am Bishop of Rome, I am happy also to extend a special greeting and affectionate thought to all Italians living and working in this country.

Good evening to everyone!

THE WORLD HAS EVER GREATER NEED OF YOUR MINISTRY

After the Mass outside Notre-Dame on May 30, the Holy Father met the Parisian clergy inside the Cathedral and addressed them as follows.

Dear brother priests,

1. It is a very great joy for me to address you already this evening—and in the first place—you priests and deacons of Paris and the Parisian region, and through you all the priests and deacons of France. For you, I am a bishop; with you, I am a priest. You are my brothers, by virtue of the sacrament of Holy Orders. The letter that I addressed to you last year for Holy Thursday told you already of my special esteem, affection and confidence. The day after tomorrow, I will have a long meeting with your bishops, who are my brothers in a special way; it is in union with them that I speak to you. But in my eyes, in the eyes of the Council, you are inseparable from the bishops; and I will think of you when I talk to them. Deep communion unites priests and bishops, based on the sacrament and the ministry. Dear friends, may you understand the love that I bear you in Christ Jesus! If Christ asks me, as He did the apostle Peter, to "strengthen my brethren," it is certainly you in the first place who must benefit from it.

2. To walk with joy and hope in our priestly life, we must go back to the sources. It is not the world that fixes our role, our status, our identity. It is Christ Jesus; it is the Church. It is Christ Jesus who chose us, as His friends, so that we may bear fruit; who made us His ministers: we take part in the task of the one Mediator, Christ. It is the Church, the Body of Christ, which, for two thousand years, has shown the indispensable place that bishops, priests and deacons have within her.

And you, priests of France, you have the fortune to be the heirs of a multitude of priests who remain examples for the whole Church, and who are for me myself a constant source of meditation. To speak only of the nearest period, I am thinking of St. Francis de Sales, St. Vincent de Paul, St. John Eudes, of the masters of the French School, of St. Louis-Mary Grignon de Montfort, St. John-Mary Vianney, and the missionaries of the nineteenth and twentieth centuries whose work I admired in Africa. The spirituality of all these pastors bears the mark of their time, but the interior dynamism is the same, and the characteristic of each one enriches the global witness of the priesthood which we have to live. How much I would have liked to go as a pilgrim to Ars, if that had been possible! The Curé of Ars remains, in fact, for all countries, a peerless model both of the accomplishment of the ministry, and of the holiness of the minister, dedicated to prayer and penitence for the conversion of souls.

Many studies and exhortations have also marked the way of the lives of priests of your country: I am thinking, for example, of the admirable letter of Cardinal Suhard: "The priest in the city." The Second

Vatican Council took up again all the doctrine of the priesthood in the Constitution *Lumen gentium* (no. 28) and in the Decree *Presbyterorum ordinis,* which had the merit of envisaging the consecration of priests in the perspective of their apostolic mission, within the People of God, and as a participation in the priesthood and in the bishop's mission. These texts are extended by many others, in particular those of Paul VI, of the Synod, and my own letter.

Those are the testimonies, those are the documents which mark out the way of the priesthood for us. This evening, in this distinguished place which is, as it were, an Upper Room, I present to you, dear friends, merely some essential recommendations.

3. In the first place, have faith in your priesthood. Oh, I am not unaware of everything that could discourage and perhaps shake certain priests today. Many analyses and testimonies stress these real difficulties which I keep well in mind—in particular the small number of ordinations—even if I do not take time to enumerate them this evening. Yet, I say to you: be happy and proud of being priests. All the baptized form a priestly people, that is, they have to offer God the spiritual sacrifice of their whole life, animated with a loving faith, uniting it with Christ's unique Sacrifice. Happy Council that reminded us of this! But precisely for this reason, we have received a ministerial priesthood to make the laity aware of their priesthood and permit them to exercise it. We have been configured to Christ the priest to be able to act on behalf of Christ the head in person (cf. Decree *Presbyterorum ordinis,* no. 2). We have been taken from among men, and we ourselves remain poor servants, but our mission as priests of the New Testament is

sublime and indispensable. It is that of Christ, the one Mediator and Sanctifier, to such an extent that it calls for the total consecration of our life and our being.

Never can the Church resign herself to lacking priests, holy priests. The more the People of God reaches its maturity, and the more Christian families and Christian laity assume their role in their multiple apostolic commitments, the more they need priests who are fully priests, precisely for the vitality of their Christian life. In another direction, the more the world is dechristianized or lacks maturity in faith, the more it, too, needs priests who are completely dedicated to bearing witness to the fullness of Christ's mystery. That is the assurance that must sustain our own priestly zeal; that is the perspective that must urge us to encourage with all our strength, through prayer, witness, appeal and training, the vocations of priests and deacons.

4. I add: apostles of Christ Jesus by the will of God (cf. beginning of all St. Paul's letters), preserve the apostolic, missionary concern, which is so deep among most French priests. Many of them—that is particularly striking in the last thirty-five years—have been haunted by the desire to proclaim the Gospel at the heart of the world, at the heart of the life of our contemporaries, in all environments, whether it is a question of intellectuals, workers, or even of the "fourth world," and also to those who are often far from the Church, who even seemed to be separated by a wall from the Church. They did so by means of new approaches of every kind, ingenious and courageous initiatives, even going to the extent of sharing the work and living conditions of workers in the perspective of the mission, in any case nearly always

with poor means. Many of them—chaplains, for example—are constantly active to meet the spiritual needs of a dechristianized, secularized world, often agitated by new cultural questionings. This pastoral concern, thought out and executed in union with your bishops, is to your honor: may it be continued and continually purified. Such is the Pope's wish. How is it possible to be a priest without sharing the zeal of the Good Shepherd? The Good Shepherd is concerned about those who are far from the flock through lack of faith or religious practice (cf. *Presbyterorum ordinis,* no. 6). With all the more reason, He is concerned about the whole flock of the faithful to be gathered and fed, as the daily pastoral ministry of so many parish priests and their assistants bears witness.

5. In this pastoral and missionary perspective, may your ministry always be that of the apostle of Jesus Christ, the priest of Jesus Christ. Never lose sight of the purpose for which you are ordained: to cause men to advance in divine life (cf. *ibid.,* no. 2). The Second Vatican Council asks you not to remain alien to the life of men and at the same time to be "witnesses and dispensers of a life other than that of this earth" (cf. *ibid.,* no. 3).

Thus, you are ministers of God's word, to evangelize and train evangelizers, to awaken, teach and nourish faith—the faith of the Church—to invite men to conversion and holiness (cf. *ibid.,* no. 4). You are associated with Christ's work of sanctification, to teach Christians to make the offering of their lives, at every moment, and especially in the Eucharist, which "appears as the source and the summit of all preaching of the Gospel" (*ibid.,* no. 5). And there, dear brother priests, we must always safeguard, with extreme care, a celebration of the Eucharist which is really worthy of this sacred mystery, as I recalled recently in my letter on this subject. Our attitude in this celebration must really make the faithful enter into this holy action, which puts them in relationship with Christ, the Holy One of God. The Church has entrusted this mystery to us, and it is she who tells us how to celebrate. You also teach Christians to imbue their whole life with the spirit of prayer; you prepare them for the sacraments; I am thinking especially of the sacrament of Penance, or reconciliation, which is of essential importance for the way of conversion of the Christian people. You are educators in the Faith, instructors of consciences, guides of souls, to enable every Christian to develop his personal vocation according to the Gospel, in sincere and active charity, to read in events what God expects of him, to take his full place in the community of Christians, which you must gather together and lead and which must be missionary (cf. *ibid.*, no. 6), and also to assume his temporal responsibilities in the human community in a manner in conformity with the Christian faith. Catechumens, the baptized, the confirmed, married couples, men and women religious, individually or in association, rely on your specific assistance to become themselves what they ought to be.

In short, all your strength is dedicated to the spiritual growth of the Body of Christ, whatever may be the precise ministry or missionary presence entrusted to you. This is your lot, which is the source of very great joy and also of very great sacrifices. You are close to all men and to all their problems "as priests." You preserve your priestly identity, which enables you to carry out the service of Christ for which you were ordained. Your priestly personality must be a sign and an indication for others; in this sense your priestly life cannot tolerate being laicized.

6. Clearly placed with regard to the laity, your priesthood is linked with that of your bishop. You take part, according to your rank, in the episcopal ministry through the sacrament of Holy Orders and the canonical mission. This is the foundation of your responsible and voluntary obedience to your bishop, your wise and trustful cooperation with him. He is the father of the presbyterium. You cannot construct the Church of God outside him. It is he who establishes the unity of pastoral responsibility, as the Pope establishes the unity in the universal Church. Reciprocally, it is with you, thanks to you, that the bishop exercises his triple function, which the Council developed at length (cf. Const. *Lumen gentium,* nos. 25-28). There is a fruitful communion there, which is not just in the field of practical coordination, but which is part of the mystery of the Church and which is emphasized particularly in the Priests' Council.

7. This unity with your bishops, dear friends, is inseparable from the unity you have to live among priests. All Christ's disciples have received the commandment of mutual love; for you, the Council goes so far as to speak of sacramental brotherhood: you participate in the same priesthood of Christ (cf. *Presbyterorum ordinis,* no. 8). Unity must be in truth: you establish the safe foundations of unity by being courageous witnesses to the truth taught by the Church in order that Christians may not be swept away by any wind of doctrine, and by carrying out all the acts of your ministry in conformity with the norms that the Church has specified, without which there would be scandal and division.

There must be unity in apostolic work, in which you are called to accept different and complementary tasks in mutual esteem and collaboration. Unity is no less necessary on the plane of brotherly love: no one must judge his brother, suspecting him *a priori* of being unfaithful, able only to criticize him, even slandering him, for which Jesus reproached the Pharisees. It is on the basis of our priestly charity that we bear witness and build up the Church. All the more so in that we have the duty, as the Council says, of leading all the laity to unity in love and to ensuring that no one feels a stranger in the community of Christians (cf. *Presbyterorum ordinis,* no. 9). In a world that is often divided, in which options are unilateral and abrupt, and methods too exclusive, priests have the noble vocation of being architects of rapprochement and unity.

8. All that, dear brothers, is connected with the experience we have of Jesus Christ, that is, holiness. Our holiness is an essential contribution to make fruitful the ministry we are carrying out (cf. *Presbyterorum ordinis,* no. 12). We are the living instruments of Christ the eternal Priest. For this purpose, we are endowed with special grace, in order to aim, for the benefit of the People of God, at the perfection of Him whom we represent. It is above all the various acts of our ministry which ordain us by themselves to this holiness: to transmit what we have contemplated, imitate what we carry out, offer ourselves entirely at Mass, lend our voice to the Church in the prayer of the hours, join in the pastoral charity of Christ... (cf. *ibid.,* nos. 12-14).

Our celibacy manifests on its part that we are entirely consecrated to the work to which the Lord has called us. The priest, seized by Christ, becomes "the man for others," completely available for the kingdom, his heart undivided, capable of accepting fatherhood in Christ. Our attachment to the person of Jesus Christ must, therefore, be strengthened in every way, by meditation on the Word, by prayer in relation to our ministry, and in the first place by the Holy Sacrifice which we celebrate every day (cf. my letter of Holy Thursday, no. 10); and it must take the means that the Church has always advised its priests to take. We must continually find again with joy the intuition of the first call that came to us from God: "Come, follow me."

9. Dear friends, I invite you to hope. I know that you bear "the burden of the day and the heat," with great merit. A list could be made of interior and exterior difficulties, subjects of anxiety, especially in this time of unbelief. No one has spoken better than the apostle Paul of the tribulations of the apostolic ministry (cf. 2 Cor. 4-5), but also of its hopes.

First and foremost, then, it is a question of faith. Do we not believe that Christ has sanctified and sent us? Do we not believe that He dwells with us, even if we bear this treasure in fragile vessels and ourselves need His mercy, whose ministers we are for others? Do we not believe that He acts through us, at least if we do His work, and that He will cause to grow what we have laboriously sown according to His Spirit? And do we not believe that He will also grant the gift of a priestly vocation to all those who will have to work with us and take over from us, especially if we ourselves are able to revive the gift we received with the laying on of hands? May God increase our faith!

Let us also extend our hope to the whole of the Church: certain members are suffering, others are in straits in many ways, others are living a real springtime. Christ must often repeat to us: "Why are you afraid, O men of little faith?" (Mt. 8:26) Christ will not abandon those who have devoted themselves to Him, those who devote themselves to Him every day.

10. This cathedral is dedicated to *Notre-Dame*. Next year, I will go to the Massabielle grotto at Lourdes, and I rejoice at this. Your country has many shrines where your faithful like to pray to the Blessed Virgin, their Mother. We priests must be the first to invoke her as our Mother. She is the Mother of the priesthood that we have received from Christ. Entrust your ministry to her, I beg you, entrust your lives to her. May she accompany you, like the first disciples, from the first joyful meeting at Cana, which makes you think of the dawn of your priesthood, to the sacrifice of the cross, which necessarily marks our lives, to Pentecost in the more and more penetrating expectation of the Holy Spirit whose Bride she has been since the Incarnation. We will end our meeting with an *Ave Maria*.

Regretfully, I must leave you, for today. But priests are always close to my heart and my prayer. In the Lord's name, I am going to bless you: bless each of you, bless the priests you represent, bless especially those who are going through a trial, physical or moral, solitude or temptation, in order that God may give His peace to everyone. May Christ be your joy! In the name of the Father, the Son and the Holy Spirit!

THE THIRST FOR HAPPINESS, A BETTER LIFE AND GOD

After his address to the clergy in Notre-Dame on May 30, John Paul II drove in an open car to the City Hall where he received the official welcome of the city from the Mayor of Paris, Mister Jacques Chirac. To the Mayor's speech of welcome, the Holy Father replied as follows.

Mr. Mayor,

I greatly appreciate the words of welcome you have just addressed to me, on behalf of the people of Paris, of its representatives, and on your own behalf. A guest of France for some days—and with what joy! —I will spend most of my stay in its marvelous capital. I have already had the happiness, on several occasions, of coming to it in the course of the past years, discovering it larger and more beautiful every time, thanks also to the efforts carried out to enhance its value. It is really one of the world capitals.

Today, Peter's Successor returns to it again not without emotion. In this Square situated a few steps from the Cité, the cradle of the town, in these places which witnessed great hours and at the same time the main vicissitudes of its history, in these places which are so symbolic in so many regards, he comes to greet the Parisian population with all the affection of his heart and all the respect merited by the glorious pages which it has inscribed in the register of time.

City of light, as it is rightly called, I hope it will remain so both for its country and for the world. It can certainly do so through the influence of its culture, and it does so. It can do so through faithfulness to its historical and artistic heritage. On many sides people look to it with as much admiration as envy; in my country of origin also, we know what we owe to Paris.

But the past is not everything. There is the present, and the present consists of very concrete questions. And there is also the future to prepare. There are these multiple problems of management and organization, which are the lot of large metropolises. But none of these problems, even from the technical aspect, is without a human element. Paris is first and foremost men and women; persons swept along by the rapid rhythm of work in offices, places of research, shops, factories; youth in search of training and employment; poor people, too, who often live their difficulties, or even their indigence, with touching dignity, and whom we can never forget; a continual coming and going of population, often uprooted; anonymous faces in which can be read the thirst for happiness, a better life and, I also believe, the thirst for the spiritual, the thirst for God.

My visit to France is a pastoral visit, as you know. As Bishop of Rome, I come up against similar situations personally every day, in my own diocese, even if the context may differ in certain points. I try in this way to understand the concern of those who are responsible, in different capacities, for the problems of a city twinned with mine, and I think I can succeed in doing so; at least I hope so.

Receive, Mr. Mayor, the fervent wishes of your guest for the heavy task that the Parisian representatives have to assume. I ask the Lord to assist you in all the efforts that will be undertaken in the service of the common good, in order that the people of Paris, so dear to my heart, may find more and more the conditions of their full development, and in this way become more and more our pride.

WITNESS TO
THE WHOLE TRUTH:
PRIMARY SERVICE
TO MANKIND

On Saturday morning, May 31, the Holy Father had a meeting in the Nunciature with the leaders of the other Christian communities. His Holiness addressed them as follows.

Dear brothers in Christ,

I thank you for this meeting which I wished to have with you during my first visit to France. First of all, I greet very cordially our Orthodox brothers, who have come mainly from different regions of the East, to live in this country which welcomed them, continuing in this way a long tradition of which Saint Irenaeus was one of the first examples. Nor do I forget the representative of the Anglican Church. And I now turn to the representatives of French Protestantism, present here.

At this stage in the effort we are making in common to restore among all Christians the unity willed by Christ, we must, indeed, become aware of the requirements that the fact of being a Christian involves for us today.

First and foremost, and in the dynamics of the movement towards unity, our personal and community memory must be purified of the memory of all the conflicts, injustice and hatred of the past. This purification is carried out through mutual forgiveness, from the depths of our hearts, which is the condition of the blossoming of real brotherly charity, a charity that is not resentful and that excuses everything (cf. 1 Cor. 13:5, 7). I say so here for I know the cruel events which, in the past, have marked the relations of Catholics with Protestants in this country. To be a Christian today requires us to forget this past in order to be wholly available for the task to which the Lord calls us now (cf. Phil. 3:13). You are facing this task and I rejoice particularly at the quality of the collaboration that exists among you, especially as regards the service of man, a service understood in its whole dimension and which requires urgently and immediately the testimony of all Christians, the necessity of which I have already stressed in the encyclical *Redemptor hominis.*

But, today, more than ever perhaps, the first service to render to man is to bear witness to the truth, the whole truth, *"alithevondes en agapi,"* "speaking the truth in love" (Eph. 4:15). We must not cease until we are once more able to confess together the whole truth, this whole truth in which the Spirit guides us (cf. Jn. 16:13). I know how frank your collaboration also is in this field, and the exchanges that took place on the occasion of the assembly of French Protestantism in 1975 are an example of this frankness. We must be able to confess the whole truth together in order to be able really to bear witness in common to Jesus Christ, the only one in whom and through whom man can be saved (cf. Acts 4:12).

I wished to tell you briefly some of the feelings that animate me at this moment, but I did not want to dwell upon the matter at greater length in order to avoid reducing the time available for more personal exchanges, and for the prayer which will conclude our meeting.

Before saying the Lord's Prayer, we could set ourselves together again before God's plan of salvation by meditating on the magnificent confession of the apostle Paul at the beginning of his letter to the Ephesians.

"Blessed be the God and Father of our Lord Jesus Christ, who has blessed us in Christ with every spiritual blessing in the heavenly places, even as he chose us in him before the foundation of the world, that we should be holy and blameless before him. He destined us in love to be his sons through Jesus Christ, according to the purpose of his will, to the praise of his glorious grace which he freely bestowed on us in the Beloved. In him we have redemption through his blood, the forgiveness of our trespasses, according to the riches of his grace which he lavished upon us. For he has made known to us in all wisdom and insight the mystery of his will, according to his purpose which he set forth in Christ as a plan for the fullness of time, to unite all things in him, things in heaven and things on earth.

"In him, according to the purpose of him who accomplishes all things according to the counsel of his will, we who first hoped in Christ have been destined and appointed to live for the praise of his glory. In him you also, who have heard the word of truth, the gospel of your salvation, and have believed in him, were sealed with the promised Holy Spirit, which is the guarantee of our inheritance until we acquire possession of it, to the praise of his glory" (Eph. 1:3-14).

Our Father, who art in heaven,
Hallowed be thy name.
Thy kingdom come,
Thy will be done,
On earth as it is in heaven.
Give us this day our daily bread;
And forgive us our trespasses,
As we forgive those who trespass against us.
And lead us not into temptation,
But deliver us from evil.
Amen.

GREAT WORK OF SPIRITUAL RENEWAL

On Saturday afternoon, May 31, the Holy Father went to the Chapel of the Miraculous Medal in Rue du Bac, where our Lady appeared in 1830 to the Sister of Charity, St. Catherine Labouré. There he recited the following prayer to Mary.

Hail Mary, full of grace, the Lord is with you, blessed are you among women, and blessed is the fruit of your womb, Jesus. Holy Mary, Mother of God, pray for us sinners, now and at the hour of our death. Amen.

O Mary conceived without sin, pray for us who have recourse to you.

This is the prayer which you inspired, O Mary, in St. Catherine Labouré, in this very place, one hundred and fifty years ago; and this invocation, now engraved on the medal, is worn and uttered by so many faithful all over the world today.

On this day when the Church celebrates the visit you paid to Elizabeth when the Son of God had already become incarnate in your womb, our first prayer will be to praise you and bless you. You are blessed among all women! Blessed are you who believed! The Almighty worked wonders for you! The wonder of your divine motherhood! And in view of it, the wonder of your Immaculate Conception! The wonder of your *Fiat!* You were so closely associated with the whole work of our Redemption, associated with the cross of our Savior; your heart was pierced by it, beside His heart. And now, in the glory of your Son, you constantly intercede for us, poor sinners. You watch over the Church whose Mother you are. You watch over each of your children. You obtain from God, for us, all these graces which are symbolized by the rays of light which radiate from your open hands. Provided only that we venture to ask you for them, that we approach you with the confidence, the boldness, the simplicity of a child. And it is in this way that you lead us incessantly towards your divine Son.

In this blessed place, I am happy to tell you again myself, today, of the trust, the very deep attachment, with which you have always graced me. *Totus tuus.* I come as a pilgrim, after all those who have come to this chapel in the last hundred and fifty years, like the whole Christian people that throngs here every day to tell you its joy, its trust, its supplication. I come like Blessed Maximilian Kolbe: before his missionary journey in Japan, exactly fifty years ago, he had come here to seek your special support to spread what he then called "the Militia of Mary Immaculate" and to undertake his marvelous work of spiritual renewal, under your patronage, before giving his life for his brothers. Today Christ asks of His Church a great work of spiritual renewal. And I, the humble Successor of Peter, come to entrust to you this great work, as I did at Jasna Gora, at Our Lady of Guadalupe, at Knock, at Pompeii, at Ephesus, and as I will do at Lourdes next year.

We dedicate to you our strength and our availability to serve the plan of salvation carried out by your Son. We pray to you that, thanks to the Holy Spirit, faith may deepen and grow stronger in the whole Christian people, that communion may triumph over all the seeds of division, that hope may be revived among those who are disheartened. We pray to you especially for this people of France, for the Church which is in France, for its Pastors, for consecrated souls, for the fathers and mothers of families, for children and the young, for men and women of the third age. We pray to you for those who are in particular distress, physical or moral, who experience the temptation of unfaithfulness, who are shaken by doubt in a climate of unbelief, and also for those who are suffering persecution because of their faith. We entrust to you the apostolate of the laity, the ministry of priests, the witness of sisters. We pray to you that the call to the priestly and religious vocation may be widely heard and followed, for the glory of God and the vitality of the Church in this country, and that of the countries which are still waiting for missionary aid.

We commend to you particularly the multitude of Daughters of Charity, whose motherhouse is established in this place and who, in the spirit of their founder, St. Vincent de Paul, and of St. Louise de Marillac are so prompt to serve the Church and the poor in all environments and in all countries. We pray to you for those who dwell in this house and who welcome, in the heart of this feverish capital, all the pilgrims who know the price of silence and prayer.

Hail, Mary, full of grace, the Lord is with you, blessed are you among women, and blessed is the fruit of your womb, Jesus. Holy Mary, Mother of God, pray for us, sinners, now and at the hour of our death. Amen.

IMITATION OF CHRIST IN CHASTITY, POVERTY, AND OBEDIENCE

In the afternoon of May 31, the Holy Father met a numerous representation of women religious of the active and contemplative life in the gardens adjoining the chapel of the Miraculous Medal in the Rue du Bac. He addressed them as follows.

My dear sisters,

1. In the course of my apostolic journeys, I feel a very deep and ever new happiness on meeting sisters, whose existence, consecrated by the three evangelical vows, "belongs undeniably to the life and holiness" of the Church (*Lumen gentium*, no. 44). Let us bless together the Lord who has permitted this meeting! Let us bless Him for the fruits it will yield in your personal lives, in your congregations, in the People of God! Thank you for having come in such large numbers from all the districts of Paris and of the Parisian region, and even from the provinces! I am happy to express to you who are here, as to all women religious of France, my esteem, my affection and my encouragement.

This gathering, in an almost rustic setting, makes me think of those moments of pause and breathing space which Christ Himself reserved for His first disciples on their return from certain apostolic tours. You too, my dear sisters, arrive from your places and tasks of evangelization: dispensaries or hospitals, day schools or boarding schools, catechetical centers or chaplaincies for the young, parish services or work in poor environments. I have pleasure in repeating to you the words of the Lord: "Come away by your-selves...and rest awhile" (cf. Mk. 6:31). Together, we will meditate on the mystery and the evangelical treasure of your vocation.

VOCATION, A GIFT OF GOD

2. Religious life is not your property, no more than it is the property of an institute. It is "a gift of God which the Church has received from her Lord and which by His grace she always safeguards" (*Lumen gentium*, no. 43). In a word, religious life is a heritage, a reality that has been lived in the Church for centuries, by a multitude of men and women. The deep experience they have made of it transcends the social and cultural differences that may exist between one country and another, surpasses also the descriptions they have left of it, and is set beyond the diversity of achievements and researches of today. It is important to listen to, and imitate, those men and women who have best embodied the ideal of evangelical perfection, and who sanctified and rendered illustrious the land of France in such large numbers.

Up to the evening of your life, remain in wonder and thanksgiving for the mysterious call that re-echoed in the depths of your heart one day: "Follow me" (cf. Mt. 9:9; Jn. 1:43); "Sell what you possess, and give it to the poor, and you will have treasure in heaven; and come, follow me" (Mt. 19:21). To begin with, you kept this call like a secret, then you subjected it to the discernment of the Church. It is, in fact, a very great risk to leave everything to follow Christ. But already you felt—and you have experienced since—that He was able to fill your hearts. Religious life is a friendship, an intimacy of the mystical order with Christ. Your personal path must be, as it were, an original re-edition of the famous poem of the Song of Solomon. Dear sisters, in the heart-to-heart relationship of prayer, absolutely vital for each of you, as on the occasion of your different apostolic commitments, listen to the Lord murmuring the same call to you: "Follow me." The ardor of your response will keep you in the freshness of your first offering. In this way you will go from faithfulness to faithfulness!

SOMETHING EXISTENTIAL

3. To follow Christ is something quite different from admiration of a model, even if you have a good knowledge of Scripture and of theology. To follow Christ is something existential. It is to want to imitate Him to the extent of letting oneself be configured to Him, assimilated to Him, to the extent of being for Him—according to the words of Sister Elizabeth of the Trinity—"an additional humanity." And that in His mystery of chastity, poverty and obedience. Such an ideal surpasses understanding and goes beyond human strength! It can be realized only thanks to special times of silent and ardent contemplation of the Lord Jesus. "Active" sisters must be at certain hours "contemplatives," following the example of the enclosed nuns whom I will address at Lisieux.

Religious chastity, my sisters, is to want really to be like Christ; all the other reasons that can be brought forward disappear before this essential reason: Jesus was chaste. This state of Christ was not only a transcending of human sexuality, foreshadowing the future world, but also a manifestation, an "epiphany" of the universality of His redeeming oblation. The Gospel shows continually how Jesus lived chastely. In His human relations, which were extraordinarily wide as compared with the traditions of His environment and His age, He reaches perfectly the deep personality of the other. His simplicity, His respect, His goodness, His art of bringing out the best in the hearts of the persons He met, overwhelm the Samaritan woman, the adulterous woman and so many other people.

May your vow of consecrated virginity—deepened and lived in the mystery of Christ's chastity and which already transfigures your persons—impel you to join in actual fact your brothers and sisters in humanity, in the concrete situations in which they find themselves! So many people in our world are, as it were, lost, crushed, desperate! In faithfulness to the rules of prudence, make them feel that you love them in the manner of Christ, drawing from His heart the human and divine tenderness that He bears them.

You have also promised Christ to be poor with Him and like Him. Certainly, the society of production and consumption raises complex problems for the practice of evangelical poverty. This is not the place or the time to discuss them. It seems to me that every congregation must see in this economic phenomenon a providential invitation to give an answer, at once traditional and new, to Christ in His poverty. It is by contemplating Him often and at length in His radically poor life, it is by frequenting assiduously the humble and the poor, who are also His face, that you will be capable of giving all that you are and all that you have. The Church needs to be borne along, as it were, by your witness. Judge your responsibility.

As for the obedience of Jesus, it has a central place in His work of redemption. You have often meditated on the pages in which St. Paul speaks of the initial disobedience, which was, as it were, the gateway to sin and death in the world, and he speaks of the mystery of Christ's obedience which starts humanity's climb back again towards God. Dispossession of oneself, humility, are more difficult for our generation enamored of autonomy and even of fantasy. It is impossible, however, to imagine religious life without obedience to superiors, who are guardians of faithfulness to the ideal of the institute. St. Paul stresses the bond of cause and effect between Christ's obedience unto death on the cross (Phil. 2:6-11) and His glory as the risen Christ and Lord of the universe. Likewise, the obedience of every sister —which is always a sacrifice of the will, out of love—yields abundant fruits of salvation for the whole world.

DO NOT BE AFRAID TO BE IDENTIFIED

4. You have agreed, therefore, to follow Christ and imitate Him more closely, to manifest His true face to those who already know Him as to those who do not know Him. And that through all these apostolic activities to which I referred at the beginning

of our meeting. On this plane of commitments, without detriment to the special spirituality of your institutes, I exhort you earnestly to seek integration in the immense network of pastoral tasks of the universal Church and the dioceses (cf. *Perfectae caritatis*, no. 20). I know that congregations cannot—for lack of subjects—answer all the appeals that come from bishops and from their priests. Do your utmost, however, to carry out the vital services of parishes and dioceses. Let duly prepared sisters collaborate in the apostolate of new situations, which are numerous. In a word, invest all your natural and supernatural talents as much as you can in contemporary evangelization. Be present, always and everywhere, in the world, without being of the world (cf. Jn. 17:15-16). Never be afraid to let your identity as women consecrated to the Lord be clearly recognized. Christians, and those who are not, have the right to know who you are. Christ, the Teacher of us all, made His life a courageous revealing of His identity (cf. Lk. 9:26).

Take heart and be confident, my dear sisters! I know that for years you have reflected a great deal on the religious life, on your constitutions. The time has come to live, in faithfulness to the Lord and to your apostolic tasks. I pray with all my heart that the witness of your consecrated lives and the aspect of your religious congregations may awaken in the hearts of many young people the project of following Christ, like you. I bless you and all women religious of France working on the soil of their homeland or in other continents. And I bless all those who are in your hearts and in your prayers.

YOUR VOICE AS EMIGRANTS PRECIOUS FOR THE FATHERLAND

After his meeting with the sisters in the Rue du Bac on Saturday afternoon, May 31, the Holy Father drove to the Champ-de-Mars where he met thousands of Polish emigrants living in Paris and in France. He spoke to them as follows in Polish.

1. I am very happy to meet the numerous French "Polish," my fellow countrymen who live in the land of France and who have come also from neighboring countries, because I know there are some among those present.

May God repay you for your presence at this particular moment. This meeting was a need of my heart and expresses our common duty to our homeland. I greet you fervently and cordially, dear brothers and sisters, and through you I greet all the sons and daughters of our country, whom destiny has led here and has linked with France.

At this meeting, therefore, I wish to bear witness to Christ before you; I wish to bear witness to you, dear brothers and sisters, and to all the generations of Poles to whose lot it has fallen to live, operate, work, fight and die here, on French soil. And I wish also to accept this testimony of the past and your contemporary and present-day witness.

May God repay you for your presence at this particular moment. This meeting was a need of my heart and expresses our common duty to our homeland.

At this meeting, therefore, I wish to bear witness to Christ before you; I wish to bear witness to you, dear brothers and sisters, and to all the generations of Poles to whose lot it has fallen to live, operate, work, fight and die here, on French soil. And I wish also to accept this testimony of the past and your contemporary and present-day witness.

I said in a speech that Paris is a place from which the whole world can be seen. Here I can say that Paris is also a place from which there can be seen, in particular, Poland, its history or at least some of its most dramatic fragments, when its destiny was decided, its "to be or not to be" on the map of the world: dramatic moments, which crushed the hearts of the generations that lived through them, but also moments that strengthened and sometimes, perhaps, even restored their sense of dignity. They consolidated and deepened the sense of national identity; they were the cry before the nation's sons and foreigners for its right to existence in the dimension of its rightful frontiers and in its framework of existence as a state.

2. The French people, which has always greatly appreciated its own freedom, has been sympathetic to others, when they found themselves in a difficult situation. Therefore here, in this land, in this city, there took place, to a considerable extent, our great national reflection, which was at the same time the reflection of faith. Although these noble desires, these great intentions and visions could not always be realized, yet here, in the different moments of history, our national ideal was renewed and the skeleton of the new religious activity, and their *raison d'être*.

Here there found refuge political refugees, patriots, thinkers, priests, writers and artists. Here many of the greatest masterpieces of our culture were born. All that is a matter of common knowledge and there is no need to lay stress on it. But, at this point, how could I fail to mention and refer with emotion at least to the Great Emigration and those who created and animated it? How could I fail to mention Mickiewicz, Norwid, Chopin? Excuse me, if I list only some names. How could I fail to recall, at this point, that here, in Paris, the Congregation of Resurrectionist Fathers was founded to save morally the emigrants and to construct Catholic Poland—as their program says. They all understood their stay in Paris as a service rendered to their country and their nation. It was the aim of their creative, political and religious activity, and their *raison d'être*.

Here, in the atmosphere of freedom, the Christian past of the nation and our Christian tradition were coined again in accordance with the necessities of the moment and the concrete situation. Here, I would say, the signs of the times of that period were read again, but read again in the light of Christ's words: "It is the Spirit that gives life" (Jn. 6:63). They tried to reawaken precisely this Spirit who gives life to man, to the nation, to the country, by supporting, developing and creating the masterpieces of Polish culture, prose, poetry, music, and art, by organizing institutions, libraries—the Polish Library here in Paris is well known and, in spite of the many difficulties it has to face, it continues this tradition and is an important cultural center in the West—and then educational and religious institutes.

But it was not only in difficult moments that Poles found the way to France and to Paris. The great and not so great architects of our culture always liked to come here and found inspiration and a favorable atmosphere.

Here the emigration was reborn morally and gained a deepened awareness of its mission of service for the homeland. So it was then, and so it must always be, because the thought of the emigration, its creative work, its contribution to the faith, culture and development of man, of Poland...of the world, is a precious and necessary supplement. If that were lacking, if this contribution, this voice were lacking, an essential thread in the complex and difficult whole would be lacking. And if Poland lives with a life of its own, if it has preserved its own culture, sovereignty and national identity, its spiritual freedom, if it has its place in the world—and, also, if a Polish Pope speaks to you today, here in Paris, the capital of France—this is also the merit of all those men who, with faith in the power of Christ's words: "It is the Spirit that gives life," defended and developed the divine and human values on which our national and Christian being is founded.

3. I apologize for having named, by necessity, only some men and some facts; there have been and are many others, no less important. I bear them all, without exception, in my heart, each one in his own place. And not only the great ones. I am thinking also of the multitude of your ancestors and fathers, simple, honest, courageous, hard-working men, who were compelled to go abroad in search of their daily bread which they had not found in their own country.

Here they found this bread; in any case, they got more of it than their own land could give them. But here, too, a difficult fate and hard work awaited them. They found themselves uprooted in a country they did not know. Hard-working and honest, they won confidence and esteem. Many of you present here bear these experiences within you. They are inscribed in your souls and on your bodies. First there were the seasonal workers, who prepared the way for permanent ones and they started emigration of the farming type. Hence hard work in the fields, in farms, in plantations. (The Polish Society of Emigrants had its centers in Paris, Soisson, Nancy.)

Another great part is the emigration of workers: Polish miners and factory workers, who settled mainly in the north of France, and there, in the coal-field basin, they were not afraid to face the hard reality and, thinking of their homeland, their family, the neighbors who had remained there, undertook the toil of daily work in the mines and factories, hoping for a better future.

In particular, in the Departments Pas de Calais, and Nord, but also Seine, Moselle, Meurthe and Moselle, Seine et Oise, Aisne and others, there are, up to today, numerous Polish colonies; you are numerous there.

And so, like your fathers, you constitute a great creative potential of the economy of this country, you make a considerable contribution to its development and progress, to its economic and spiritual power, in conformity with the words of the prophet Jeremiah: "Seek the welfare of the city where I have sent you into exile, and pray to the Lord on its behalf, for in its welfare you will find your welfare" (29:7).

I am thinking of the generation that found itself outside its homeland, owing to the terrible events of the second world war. A generation that did not hang up its lyres on the willows of that land in a tragic hour of history.

4. I am thinking with gratitude of so many Polish priests, who have served and serve the emigrants with sacrifice and dedication through thick and thin. Thanks to them, Polish emigrants did not lose the Faith. In spite of various difficulties and obstacles, it

was precisely they who contributed to a large extent to preserve their identity, their language, links with their native land, drawing inspiration and seeking support in the native and Christian culture of Poland.

How could I fail to mention here also the Major Seminary in Rue des Irlandais? It carries out an important role in pastoral work, in the preparation of Polish pastors of souls with the nourishment of the spirit. On this occasion, I wish to express my gratitude to the Church in Ireland, which has been so understanding in meeting the needs of the Polish apostolate for emigrants and has facilitated their use of the building in which they work.

I am thinking of so many organizations and associations among emigrants, which seek inspiration for their activity in faith in God. One of them, the Catholic Association of Polish Youth, is just celebrating its fiftieth anniversary. With special love, but also with solicitude—because I know your difficulties and the threats that hang over you—I am thinking of you young people, of all you boys and girls, and I will say to you just what I have already said on many occasions to so many young people: you are the generation of the Church and her future, you are the hope of the country in which you live, of the world, of Euro-emigration, of the country of your ancestors, you are my hope. Do not give in to complexes, do not cut that root from which you have grown. Learn how to read what is in you and around you. Learn to read, to discern and choose.

Integration is certainly an important and necessary problem for you all. Today no one can shut himself up in his own ghetto. You must serve the country in which you live, work for it, love it and con-

I am thinking of you young people, of all you boys and girls, and I will say to you just what I have already said on many occasions to so many young people: you are the generation of the Church and her future, you are the hope of the country in which you live, of the world, of Euro-emigration, of the country of your ancestors; you are my hope. Do not give in to complexes, do not cut that root from which you have grown. Learn how to read what is in you and around you. Learn to read, to discern and choose.

tribute to its progress, developing yourselves, your humanity, what is in you, and forms you, without distorting or cancelling those lines that go backwards and, through your parents and the generations, perhaps many already, are rooted in a reality more modest and poorer than the one in which you live to-day, but great and precious. Do not let yourselves be deceived by easy words, current expressions, super-ficial opinions. Read this reality, learn it, love it, transform it and give it a new, modern dimension. To know it and live it in daily life often helps to under-stand oneself and the other, helps to approach God by means of faith and love.

The measure of the things and events of the created world is man, but the measure of man is God. Therefore, man must always return to this source, to this one measure, which is God incarnate in Jesus Christ, if he wants to be a man, and if the world is to be human. It is precisely to this fundamental and most important truth that I wish to bear witness with this visit of mine to France and at this meeting with you today, dear brothers and sisters. Return to this truth, meditate upon it, and in it you will again find yourselves and others, all the vicissitudes that make up human life as a whole, your concrete life and your tasks in all directions. In the meantime, Christ be-longs to us, insofar as we make ours His teaching, His salvific message of love. Grow and increase your faith, hope and charity. I address this appeal to you with special forcefulness.

Now let us all, you and I, turn our thoughts and our hearts to Jasna Gora, to the Mother of Christ and of every man, to the Mother and Queen of Poland, and let us entrust to her ourselves, your families, your fathers and mothers, husbands and wives, sons and daughters, your priests and parishes, your neighbors, the Church in our country and all over the world, and France with which God has linked your life.

From the depths of my heart I impart the apostolic blessing to all of you present here, to your families, and to all those who are united with us in affection, thought and prayer.

SINCERE EFFORT
AT UNDERSTANDING

Before the celebrated Mass on the evening of Saturday, May 31, in the Basilica of Saint-Denis, John Paul II met some representatives of the Muslim community of France and spoke to them as follows.

It is with great joy that I address my greeting to you Muslims, our brothers in faith in the one God. Through you, I greet all your brothers and sisters who also live in this country.

If the reason that has led you to leave your respective countries, whether it be work or study, gives your step a character of unquestionable dignity, it is nevertheless true that your condition as emigrants raises for you, as it does for this country that receives you, important social, cultural and religious problems.

I know that efforts have been undertaken to understand your problems and to seek satisfactory solutions, and I am thinking here in particular of the many socio-professional and cultural organizations which are aware of your situation, as well as that of other immigrants living in France.

The Church, too, is conscious of it. I will mention only two initiatives that she has taken: the conciliar declaration of October 28, 1965, in which she not only affirmed her will to seek dialogue with Islam, but "urges...for the benefit of all men, let them together preserve and promote peace, liberty, social justice and moral values," and the creation on May 19, 1964, of the "Secretariat for Non-Christians." I recently affirmed this desire of the Church in the course of my journey in Africa, on meeting representatives of Islam at Nairobi and Accra. This concern on the plane of the universal Church finds an expression nearer to you in the "Secretariat for Relations with Islam," set up by the Church in France.

However, I am aware that not all your problems are solved, no more than those of other workers in the world, no more than those of many Christians who live and work in a certain number of Muslim countries. But we are convinced that the good will, the sincere effort of understanding and the common pursuit of solutions in a real desire of reconciliation may, with the assistance of the one God in whom we all believe, help to find satisfactory solutions.

Our common ideal is a society in which men recognize one another as brothers who walk in the light of God in emulation for good.

Thank you for your presence here.

VOCATION TO LOVE AND TO JUSTICE EXPRESSED IN WORK

On Saturday evening, May 31, the Holy Father concelebrated Mass in the Basilica of Saint-Denis in the working-class sector on the outskirts of Paris. The Basilica was packed to capacity, and the Mass was relayed by loudspeakers to the hundreds of thousands outside in the Square. After the Gospel the Pope went outside the church and preached his homily which was relayed to those in the Basilica.

1. "Blessed are you..."

Allow me, dear brothers and sisters gathered within and around this venerable basilica of Saint-Denis which shelters the tombs of the kings of France, to greet with you Mary, the Mother of Christ.

You know the words of this greeting. You have certainly uttered them more than once, or you have heard others uttering them:

"Blessed are you among women,
and blessed is the fruit of your womb" (Lk. 1:42).

A greeting which is addressed to a woman bearing in her womb a man: the fruit of life and the beginning of life. This woman comes from far away, from Nazareth, and now she is entering the house of her relatives, whom she has come to visit. From the threshold of the house, she hears: "Blessed is she who believed that there would be a fulfillment of what was spoken to her from the Lord!" (Lk. 1:45)

On the last day of the month of May, the Church remembers this visit and these words: she greets Mary, the Mother of Jesus Christ. She does honor to her maternity, whereas the latter is still only a mystery in her womb and her heart.

I wish, in the first place, to do honor to maternity, and to the faith in man that it implies. I then wish to pay tribute to man's work, this work through which man provides a living for his relatives, his family first of all—this family has, therefore, fundamental rights —this work through which man realizes his vocation to love, for the world of human work is constructed on moral power, on love. It is love that must inspire justice and the struggle for justice.

DIGNITY OF MAN

2. To do honor to maternity means accepting man in his full truth and in his full dignity, and that from the very beginning. Man's beginning is in his mother's womb.

At this great gathering, in which mainly workers participate, I would like to greet every man, every woman, by virtue of the great dignity which is his from the first moment of existence in his mother's womb. Everything that we are finds its beginning there.

The first measure of man's dignity, the first condition of respect for the inviolable rights of the human person, is the honor due to the mother. It is the cult of maternity. We cannot detach man from his human beginning. Today when we have learned so much about the biological mechanisms which, in their respective fields, determine this beginning, we must, with all the keener awareness and all the more ardent conviction, proclaim the human—deeply human—beginning of every man as the fundamental value and the basis of all his rights. The first right of man is the right to life. We must defend this right and this value. In the contrary case, the whole logic of faith in man, the whole program of really human progress, would be shaken and collapse.

On the threshold of the house of Zachariah, Elizabeth said to Mary: Blessed are you, you who believed (cf. Lk. 1:45). Let us do honor to maternity, because faith in man is expressed in it. I feel an additional joy in doing so on this eve of the feast that all French families dedicate to mothers. The act of faith in man is the fact that his parents give him life. The mother bears him in her womb, and she is ready to suffer all the pains of childbirth; thereby, with all her feminine self, with all her maternal self, she proclaims her faith in man. She bears witness to the value which is in her and transcends her at the same time, to the value constituted by the one who, still unknown, just conceived, fully hidden in his mother's womb, must be born and be manifested to the world as a son of his parents, as a confirmation of their humanity, as a fruit of their love, as a future of the family: of the closest family, and at the same time of the whole human family.

This child will perhaps be weak, maladjusted; he will perhaps be deficient. It sometimes happens in this way. Maternity is always pain—the love for which one pays with one's suffering—and it happens that this love may have to be even greater than the pain of childbirth itself. This pain may be extended to the whole life of the child. The value of humanity is confirmed also by these children and by these men in whom it is retarded and sometimes undergoes a painful degradation....

This is a further element to affirm that it is not enough to define man according to all the bio-physiological criteria, and that it is necessary to believe in man, from the beginning.

Blessed are you, Mary, you who believed! The one you bear in your heart, as the fruit of your womb, will come into the world in the night of Bethlehem. He will then proclaim the Gospel to men, and He will be raised on the cross. It was for that purpose, in fact, that He came into the world, to bear witness to the truth. In Him there will be manifested to the end the truth about man, the mystery of man, his ultimate and highest vocation: the vocation of every man, even of the man whose humanity will not, perhaps, reach a complete and normal development; of every man without exception, not stopping at any consideration of qualification or at degrees of intelligence, sensitiveness or physical performance, but by virtue of his very humanity, owing to the fact that he is a man. Because, thanks to that, thanks to his humanity itself, he is the image and likeness of the infinite God.

THIS WORKING CLASS
DISTRICT OF PARIS

3. I know that in this assembly it is mainly workers who are listening to me. Today this district, round its ancient basilica, has become one of the most working class districts in the Parisian suburbs. And I know that many workers, Frenchmen and foreigners,

live and work here, often under precarious conditions as regards housing, wages and jobs. I think also of the French population from beyond the seas. An important number of their sons work here, at Paris: they represent it among us. I am thinking in a special way of those who have come from far away, from Portugal, Spain, Italy, Poland, Yugoslavia, Turkey, North Africa, Mali, Senegal, Southeast Asia. In spite of the efforts that have been made for them and the welcome they are given in this country, there is thus necessarily added to the worker's hard life an uprooting which is all the more painful in that the family is sometimes split up between the country of origin and the country of work. There is also the suffering of an anonymity which may make people feel homesick for the emotional warmth of their native town or village.

Yes, this present-day urban life makes human relations difficult, in the hectic rush, never ended, between the place of work, the family lodging and the shopping centers. The integration of the children, of the young, of the old, often raises acute problems. They are so many appeals to work together to create more and more human conditions of life for everyone! The presence of migrants is, moreover, a source of fruitful exchange on both sides.

I am anxious above all to encourage the Christian apostolate which is carried out in a real concern for evangelization by priests, sisters, young and adult lay people, all devoted to this working class world.

I shall now tackle a difficult reflection on man's work and on justice. Let all those whose lives I have just evoked rest assured that I keep in mind their situation, their efforts, and that I wish to manifest all my affection to them as well as to their families.

4. There exists a close connection, there exists a particular connection between man's work and the fundamental environment of human love, which bears the name of the family.

Man has been working from the beginning to subdue the earth and dominate it. We take this definition of work from the first chapters of the Book of Genesis. Man works to earn his living and that of his family. We take this definition of work from the Gospel, from the life of Jesus, Mary and Joseph, and also from everyday experience. These are the fundamental definitions of human work. They are both authentic, that is, fully humanistic, and the second one contains a particular fullness of the Gospel content.

WILLED BY THE CREATOR

These fundamental contents must be followed to ensure man an adequate place in the economic order as a whole. It is easy, in fact, to lose this place. It is lost when work is envisaged, above all, as one of the elements of production, as a "merchandise" or an "instrument." The name of the systems on which this position is based is not important: if man is subordinated to production, if he becomes merely its instrument, then work, human work, is deprived of its dignity and its specific meaning. We are happy to remember here Cardinal Cardijn's famous words: "A young worker is worth more than all the gold in the world."

That is why, among the different measures that make it possible to evaluate man's work, the measure of the family must be put in the foreground. When man works to provide for his family's subsistence, that means that he puts all the daily toil of love into his work. For it is love that brings the family into being, it is love that is its constant expression, its stable environment. Man can also love work for work's sake, because it enables him to participate in the great work of dominating the earth, the work willed by the Creator. And this love, certainly, corresponds to man's dignity. But the love that man puts into his work finds its full measure only if he connects it up, if he unites it with men themselves, and above all, with those who are his own flesh and blood.

Work, therefore, cannot destroy the family: on the contrary, it must unite it, help it to perfect its cohesion. The rights of the family must be deeply inscribed in the very foundations of every code of work, since the latter has as its subject man, and not just production and profit. How, for example, can a satisfactory solution be found for the problem—similar in many countries—of the woman who works in a factory, at a tiring pace, and who is constantly concerned about being with her children and her husband?

I evoke here a vast program, which could be the object of many specialized studies to exhaust all its content. I will confine myself to some aspects which seem to me to be of vital importance. In the course of my life, I had the luck, the divine grace, to be able to discover these fundamental truths about human work, thanks to my personal experience of manual work. I shall remember as long as I live the men with whom I was linked in the same workyard, whether in the stone quarries or in the factory. I shall not forget the human kindness that my fellow workers showed towards me. I shall not forget the discussions we had, in free moments, on the fundamental problems of ex-

In the course of my life, I had the luck, the divine grace, to be able to discover these fundamental truths about human work, thanks to my personal experience of manual work. I shall remember as long as I live the men with whom I was linked in the same workyard, whether in the stone quarries or in the factory. I shall not forget the human kindness that my fellow workers showed towards me. I shall not forget the discussions we had, in free moments, on the fundamental problems of existence and of the life of workers. In my experience of life, I learned what a worker is, and I bear that in my heart.

istence and of the life of workers. I know what value their home, the future of their children, the respect due to their wives, to their mothers, had for these men, who were at the same time fathers of families. From this experience of some years, I drew the conviction and the certainty that man expresses himself in work as a subject capable of loving, oriented towards fundamental human values, ready for solidarity with every man....

In my experience of life, I learned what a worker is, and I bear that in my heart. I know that work is also a necessity, sometimes a dire necessity; and yet man wishes to transform it to measure up to his dignity and his love. His grandeur lies in that. Very often, living conditions force men to leave their country to go in search of work, as is the case for many of you. It is to be hoped that every society will be capable of giving its own citizens enough work! If, however, emigration for reasons of work becomes a need or a necessity, I trust all the more that all those who find themselves in this situation will be able to transform this necessity to measure up to the love that ties them to their dear ones: to their families, to their native countries. It is false to say that the worker has no country. He is, in fact, in a special way, the representative of his people, he is the man of his own house. In human work are inscribed above all the law of love, the need of love, the order of love.

Today's liturgy itself speaks of it, using the words of the apostle Paul who, as is known, lived by the work of his hands: "Hate what is evil, hold fast to what is good; love one another with brotherly affection.... Rejoice in your hope, be patient in tribulation, be constant in prayer...practice hospitality.... Rejoice with those who rejoice, weep with those who weep. Live in harmony with one another'' (Rom. 12:9-16).

MAN HUNGERS FOR TRUTH AND FREEDOM

5. The world of human work must, therefore, be above all a world constructed on moral strength: it must be the world of love, and not the world of hatred. It is the world of construction and not that of destruction. The rights of man, of the family, of the nation, of mankind, are deeply inscribed in human work. The future of the world depends on respect for them.

Does that mean that today the fundamental problem of the world of work is not justice and the struggle for social justice? On the contrary: it means that there is no means of detaching the reality of human work from this justice and this noble struggle.

Does not the liturgy of today, on the feast of the Visitation of Mary, speak about it in a certain way too? Does not the truth about the justice of God ring out at the same time as the worship of God, whose mercy is for all generations, in the words that the evangelist St. Luke put into the mouth of the Virgin, who bears in her womb the Son of God? ''He has shown strength with his arm, he has scattered the proud in the imagination of their hearts, he has put down the mighty from their thrones, and exalted those of low degree; he has filled the hungry with good things, and the rich he has sent empty away'' (Lk. 1:51-53).

These words tell us that the world willed by God is a world of justice. That the order that must govern relations between men is based on justice. That this order must be continually realized in the world, and even that it must always be realized anew, as situations and social systems grow and develop, in proportion to new conditions and economic possibilities, new possibilities of technology and production, and at the same time new possibilities and necessities of distributing goods.

These words of Mary's *Magnificat* are uttered in the finest outburst of gratitude to God, who—as Mary proclaims—has done great things in her. They say that the world willed by God cannot be a world in which some, few in number, accumulate excessive goods in their hands, and the others—who are clearly superior in number—suffer from want, poverty and die of hunger.

Who are the former? And who are the others? Is it a question only of two social classes opposed to each other? Here we must not confine ourselves in too narrow schemata. It is a question today, in fact, of whole societies, of whole areas of the world, which have already been defined in different ways. We talk, for example, of developed societies and underdeveloped societies. But we must also speak of consumer societies, and of those in which men are literally dying of starvation. Today it is necessary to have a very wide, universal view of the problem as a whole. Closed schemata are not sufficient. These narrow schemata can sometimes, on the contrary, obstruct the road more than clear it, for example, when it is a question of the victory of a system or a party more than of man's real needs.

These needs exist, however, not only in the field of economy, and in the field of the distribution of material goods. There exist other real human needs, there exist also other human rights which are subject to violence. And not only the rights of man, but also the rights of the family and the rights of nations. "Man shall not live by bread alone..." (Mt. 4:4). He is not only hungry for bread, he is hungry, perhaps even more, for truth. He is hungry for freedom, when some of his fundamental rights are violated, such as the right to freedom of conscience and to religious freedom, the right to the education of his children in conformity with the faith and convictions of parents and families, the right to instruction according to capacities and not, for example, according to a political situation or a conception of the world imposed by force.

JUSTICE, THE CONDITION OF PEACE

6. The world of human work, the great society of workers, if they are constructed particularly on moral power—and it should be so!—must consequently remain sensitive to all these dimensions of injustice which have developed in the modern world. They must be capable of struggling nobly for every form of justice: for the real good of man, for all the rights of the person, of the family, of the nation, of mankind. This justice is the condition of peace, as Pope John XXIII expressed with deep insight in his encyclical *Pacem in terris*. Readiness to undertake such a noble struggle, a struggle for the real good of man in all his dimensions, is derived from the words spoken by Mary when she bears Christ in her womb, spoken about the living God, when she says:

"He has shown strength with his arm,
he has scattered the proud in the imagination
of their hearts,
he has put down the mighty from their thrones,
and exalted those of low degree;
he has filled the hungry with good things,
and the rich he has sent empty away"
(Lk. 1:51-53).

Christ will say one day: "Blessed are those who hunger and thirst for righteousness, for they shall be satisfied" (Mt. 5:6). However, this thirst for righteousness, this eagerness to struggle for truth and moral order in the world, are not and cannot be hate, or a source of hate in the world. They cannot be turned into a program of struggle against man, solely because he is, if one may express it so, "on the other side." This struggle cannot become a program of destruction of the adversary, it cannot create social and political mechanisms in which there are manifested ever greater forms of collective egoism, powerful and destructive egoism, egoism which sometimes destroys its own society, and its own nation, which also destroys others unscrupulously—nations and societies that are weakest from the point of view of human and economic potential and civilization—by depriving them of their independence and their real sovereignty, and by exploiting their resources.

THREAT OF NUCLEAR DESTRUCTION

Our modern world witnesses the increase of the terrible threat of the destruction of men by other men, especially with the accumulation of nuclear weapons. Already the cost of these weapons and the threatening atmosphere they bring about have caused millions of men and entire populations to see reduced their possibilities of bread and of freedom. Under these conditions, the great society of workers, precisely in the name of the moral power with which it is endowed, must demand categorically and clearly: where, in what field, why, have the bounds of this noble struggle been overstepped, the struggle for the good of man, in particular the most underprivileged and the neediest? Where, in what field, why, has this moral and creative power been turned into a destructive force, hatred in the new forms of collective selfishness in which glimpses can be caught of the threat of the possibility of a struggle of all against all, and of a monstrous self-destruction?

Our age demands that we should ask ourselves these questions, such fundamental questions. It is a categorical imperative of consciences: of every man, whole societies, and, in particular, of those on whom the main responsibility weighs for the present and for the future of the world. It is in this question that is manifested the moral power which is represented by the worker, by the world of work, and at the same time by all men.

We must ask ourselves once more: in the name of what right have this moral power, this readiness to struggle for truth, this hunger and thirst for righteousness, been systematically—and even in programs—detached from the words of the Mother who venerates God with her whole soul while she bears the Son of God in her womb? For what reason has the struggle for righteousness in the world been linked with the program of a radical denial of God? With the organized program of the atheistic impregnation of men and societies?

It must be asked, if not for other reasons, at least in the name of the complete truth about man. In the name of his interior freedom and his dignity. And also in the name of his whole history.

That is a question that must be asked.

WORKING IN A DYNAMISM OF LOVE

In any case, Christians cannot, do not want to, prepare this world of truth and righteousness in hate, but only in the dynamism of love.

To conclude, let us ever be mindful of the words of today's liturgy: "Let love be genuine; hate what is evil, hold fast to what is good; love one another with brotherly affection; outdo one another in showing honor. Never flag in zeal, be aglow with the Spirit, serve the Lord. Rejoice in your hope" (Rom. 12:9-12).

With an affectionate greeting and best wishes, I likewise exhort the beloved emigrants who speak Portuguese, to be faithful to the real values of the family as God wills it and of honored work. And that, although living conditions are difficult: I summon them to their Christian vocation and to the worthy traditions of which they are bearers, even outside their beloved country. And may our Lady be for all a light and example to follow and, as Mother of our trust, obtain for them assistance, comfort and grace from God!

I now wish to address a particularly cordial greeting, in their own language, to the Spanish emigrants who are taking part in this event.

I know very well the problems and difficulties you have to face up to in your life, in foreign surroundings and not infrequently in a situation of isolation. Show mutual solidarity, helping one another to maintain and promote your dignity as men and sons of God. And do not forget the Christian values you received from your ancestors.

With my respect and affectionate esteem for you, your children and families, I ask the Lord to bless you always.

ADEQUATE RESPONSE
TO THE NEEDS
OF SOCIETY TODAY

*On his return to the Nunciature in the late evening of May 31,
the Holy Father met the leaders of the various lay apostolate
movements. After listening to their reports he addressed them as
follows.*

Dear friends,

1. I am very happy to meet this evening the national leaders of the lay apostolate movements. Beyond yourselves, I cordially greet and encourage all members of your associations and their chaplains.

As your simple presentation shows, the lay apostolate in France is flourishing in a very great variety. I know that it is not just the typically Cartesian genius of distinguishing the different aspects of things that urges your fellow countrymen in this direction, but far more the concern to respond as well as possible both to the differentiated tasks of the Church, and to situations of life and age, as well as social and professional backgrounds. Thus revision of life can gain in precision and action in deep efficacy. I recognize in this the sign of a dynamism and riches on which I congratulate you.

2. Each movement pursues its aim, with its own methods, in its sector or its environment, but it is

important, however, to become aware of your complementarity and to establish links between the movements: not just mutual esteem, a dialogue, but a certain concerted action and even real collaboration. You are called to do so in the name of your common Faith, in the name of your common membership of the People of God, and more precisely of the same local Church, in the name of the same essential goals of the apostolate, faced with the same problems with which the Church and society have to deal. Yes, it is salutary to become aware that the specialization of your movements generally makes it possible to grasp in depth one aspect of realities, but that it calls for other complementary forms of apostolate.

Moreover, you can never forget that, in addition to your associations, there is a whole people of baptized and confirmed persons, "practicing" faithful who, without enrolling in a movement, carry out personally a real Christian apostolate, an ecclesial apostolate, in their families, in their little communities, especially in their parishes, through their example and by dedication to multiple apostolic tasks. How could I fail to mention here the fine service of catechesis to which so many of the laity of France devote part of their heart and their time, and which calls, moreover, for ongoing formation?

MULTIPLE TASKS

In short, the action of your movement takes place in a whole, and I know that many of you, moreover, are anxious to arrange opportunities for meeting with other movements or with other Christians engaged in the apostolate, for example, at the level of the parish, at the level of the diocese—the pastoral council should help in this matter—and on the national plane: is it not one of the roles of the Secretariat of the Lay Apostolate? In any case, this evening a marvelous opportunity is offered us to gather in your persons a large part of the organized laity, and that is a symbol of your vocation to work together, to live in communion.

CHURCH HAS NEED OF LAITY APOSTOLATE

3. Not being able, unfortunately, to reserve a special word for each movement or group of movements, I will merely stress some perspectives which are an integral part of the foundations and orientations of every association of Christians: your vocation as lay people, your work of evangelization, your Catholic identity, your ecclesial membership, your prayer.

In the first place, is it necessary to repeat to you how much the Church—and the Pope in her name—counts on your apostolate as laity? The work which falls specifically to you in the Church is essential. No one can replace you, neither priests, nor sisters, whom I do not fail, as you know, to encourage in their specific role. Preachers and educators in the Faith, the priests are there to help you to impregnate your lives with the spirit of the Gospel and to unite the spiritual offering of your lives with that of Christ. Their role is indispensable and you must be greatly concerned, you too, about priestly vocations. Likewise men and women religious are there to bear witness to the beatitudes and to undivided love of Christ. I ask them to act as priests, as religious; and you must act as real laity, responsible day in and day out for the family, social and professional tasks in which you in-carnate the presence and the witness of Christ, in which you try to make this world and its structures a world more worthy of the sons of God.

In this way you develop as Christians all your capacities as men; and likewise women, who have a magnificent role to play in the apostolate today, with all the resources of their femininity, in a world in which they have and take their place and accept their responsibilities to an ever increasing extent. In short, you all take part in the mission of the Church, in its prophetic, priestly and royal mission, by virtue of your baptism and your confirmation.

Happy Vatican II which highlighted your "voca-tion as laity," linking it up with the life of the People of God as a whole! There is no need for me to mention to you the Constitution *Lumen gentium* (nos. 30-38) or the Decree *Apostolicam actuositatem* which must remain the charter of your rights and duties in the Church.

At Krakow, we worked together in synod, for years, with the laity, in order to assimilate the Coun-cil better and to live it. I was also, through the benevo-lence of Paul VI, a member of the Pontifical Council for the Laity. And in Rome, I try to take the time to receive groups of lay people as much as possible.

I have taken the liberty of stressing your noble role, your indispensable role, whereas you are quite convinced of it, and, probably, your movements still experience vitality and encouraging fruits. But I know also the difficulties that your apostolate meets with today. They come from the world that you want to evangelize: it is strongly marked by secularization, let us say even by unbelief, and also by the dulling of the moral sense, not counting the acute problems raised by certain living conditions and social changes. But the difficulties may also affect your movements themselves and their members, owing, for example, to greater hesitation to commit themselves at present, or else because certain movements have experienced weariness and deviations, perhaps because they have neglected one of the elements about which I am going to speak. But, in spite of all that, the organized apostolate which is entrusted to you, without denying the place of other forms of apostolate, is still today an instrument, the importance of which for evangelization must not be underestimated.

EVANGELIZATION HOLDS FIRST PLACE

4. *Evangelization* is, in fact, the common purpose of all your movements. It is by definition the guiding thread of your programs of Catholic Action or movements of spirituality; but it is also true for Christian movements of cultural activities and socio-charitable movements, for it is a question, in a word, of carrying out a work of Christian education or bearing witness to God's tenderness and forming hearts to charity.

The whole Apostolic Exhortation *Evangelii nuntiandi* of my Predecessor, Paul VI, illustrates magnificently the meaning and the ways of evangelization. You are called to be witnesses of the Good News of salvation in Jesus Christ, to contribute to the conversion of the personal and collective conscience of men. In this way you enable them to live as a Church —which involves witness of life, explicit proclamation, catechesis, sacramental and community life, education to Christian commitment—and, moreover, you impregnate the world with the values of the Gospel in the perspective of the kingdom of God. Your apostolate, therefore, proclaims Jesus Christ at the heart of family, professional, social and political life; it guides the efforts made to create better living conditions, more in conformity with justice, peace, truth and brotherhood. But the witness of your movements cannot be confused with a technical, economic or political work. It aims, in fact, at "making the whole of creation new.... But there is no new humanity if there are not first of all new persons renewed by Baptism and by lives lived according to the Gospel" *(Evangelii nuntiandi,* no. 18), according to justice, peace and love of Christ.

TO STRENGTHEN YOUR IDENTITY

5. This exalting and demanding mission requires the members of your movements to strengthen their *Christian and Catholic identity* continually, without which they could not be the witnesses of whom we have spoken. Certainly, the apostolic dialogue involves the effort of looking at and analyzing carefully the realities lived by our contemporaries: but at the same time it always calls for critical discernment to separate the wheat from the tares. The apostolic dialogue calls us to recognize the toothing-stones and even the signs of the Holy Spirit at work in the heart of persons; but that presupposes precisely the look of deep faith, and concern for purification and a revelation in fullness. That is why I deeply approve all the efforts your movements are making to encourage a deepening of the faith, thanks to doctrinal reflection

on Christ, the Church, man redeemed by Christ; and a real spiritual effort. For, in a word, the apostolic dialogue starts from the faith and presupposes a firm Christian identity. That is all the more necessary, as you experience, since your apostolic activity plunges you into a more secularized world, since the questions raised are more delicate, and those who offer to serve in your movements today are, in spite of their great generosity, less assured in the Faith, less supported by Christian structures, and more sensitive to ideologies alien to faith.

BECOMING MORE AWARE

6. You cannot strengthen your Catholic identity without strengthening your membership of the People of God, in its practical implications. That means being aware that our whole Christian being comes to us through the Church: faith, divine life, sacraments, life of prayer; that the centuries-old experience of the Church nourishes us and helps us to walk along ways that are partly new; that the Magisterium is given to the Church to guarantee her authenticity, her unity and her 'consistent and safe operation. Even more than that, I hope that your laity will learn to love the Church as a Mother, to be happy and proud to be her sons and active members. As I was saying to you at the beginning, the ecclesial spirit must make you seek dialogue and collaboration with other associations, with the whole People of God, from whom you cannot be separated and in whose service you are. I called you, furthermore, to assume your responsibility as lay people: it is necessarily linked up with that of the priest who must keep his place, in your teams, as a

priest, as a sign of Christ the Head, taking part in His mediation, and a sign of the Church which always extends beyond the life of the team or the movement.

Moreover, as national leaders at the head of your movements, you will be able to combine unity of program and action with the flexibility that permits an adapted and responsible action at all levels. Above all your movements will have at heart to enter the perspectives of the local Church, of the universal Church, through your trusting communion with your bishops and with Peter's Successor. I know and appreciate that at the national level this bond is manifested especially with the bishops of the episcopal commissions specialized in your problems.

PERSONS OF PRAYER

7. I conclude with the encouragement to be men and women of prayer. For it is the Spirit of God that must be the soul of your apostolate, impregnate your thoughts, your desires, your actions, purify them and elevate them. The laity are called like priests and religious to holiness; prayer is its special way. And then you have many opportunities to give thanks and to intercede for those with whom you come into contact. I have learned with great pleasure that there is in France a real renewal of prayer, which is expressed among other ways by the flourishing of prayer groups, but which affects also, I hope, the life of your movements. God be praised! May the Blessed Virgin always accompany the apostolate you are undertaking on the behalf of her Son. And I, expressing to you my trust and joy, bless you willingly as well as all the members of your movements, and your families.

"Hail Mary, full of grace,
the Lord is with you,
blessed are you among women,
and blessed is the fruit of your womb, Jesus.
Holy Mary, Mother of God,
pray for us sinners,
now and at the hour of our death.
Amen."

TRUTHS ABOUT MAN AND GOD ARE INSEPARABLE

On Sunday, June 1, John Paul II met the professors and students of the Catholic Institute, where he himself, as a young priest, had been a student in the Canon Law Faculty. After an address of homage by the Rector, Most Reverend Paul Poupard, Auxiliary Bishop of Paris, the Holy Father spoke as follows.

Most Reverend Rector,

1. I thank you heartily for your words of welcome, as I thank also with all my heart all those who surround me this morning for this reception which touches me deeply. In my turn, I address to you my most cordial greeting, as well as to the high personalities who have kindly wished to accept your invitation and who honor this meeting with their presence. I greet all the members of the University community whom I am particularly happy to meet in this place, the heir to the most impressive University tradition. In this setting, so evocative and so pregnant with history, you will allow me, I am sure, Your Excellency, ladies and gentlemen, to reflect, as a former professor, and address especially those for whom the Catholic Institute exists: its students.

2. Dear friends, the situation that is yours, here in Paris, calls for reflection on the profound reasons for your presence in this Institute. Is not the university world of Paris, illustrious for so many reasons, rich in competences of all orders, literary and scientific? In how many centers could you not find, with learning

and love of truth, the foundation of that intellectual freedom without which there cannot be, anywhere, either the university spirit or a university worthy of the name?

However, the magnificent scientific development of the modern age has also its weaknesses, of which almost exclusive attachment to the natural sciences and their technical applications, is not the least. Is not humanism itself often reduced to loving cultivation of the great testimonies of the past without finding again their roots? Finally, the human sciences, the fundamental discoveries of our age, also bear within them, in spite of the horizons they open up to us, the limits inherent in their methodological models and their premises.

At the same time, how many persons are in search of a truth capable of unifying their lives? A moving search, even when the appeal of the fundamental values inscribed in the deepest recesses of their being is suffocated, as it were, by the influence of the environment. The search is often an anxious one: many are "groping," like the Athenians addressed by St. Paul, for the God that we proclaim to them. All the more so since the upheavals of our age manifest before our eyes, in many respects, the more and more obvious failure of all the forms of what can be called "atheistic humanism."

3. I do not think I am mistaken, then, when I say that the students ask of the Catholic Institute of Paris, at the same time as the various branches of knowledge that are offered to them and through them, personal access to another order of truth, the complete truth about man, inseparable from the truth about God such as He revealed it to us, for it can come only

from the Father of lights, from the gift of the Holy
Spirit, He who, the Lord assured us, would lead us to
the entire truth.

That is why, although your Institute has also
distinguished itself in the university world through
the work of eminent men in the different branches of
learning, it is not knowledge as such that justifies in
the first place your belonging to the Catholic Institute,
but the light it contributes to offer you about your
reasons for living. In this field, every man needs certainty. We Christians find it in the mystery of Christ
who is, in His own words, our Way, our Truth, our
Life. It is he who is at the starting point of our
spiritual quest, He is its soul. He will be its goal. Thus,
religious knowledge and spiritual progress go hand-
in-hand. St. Augustine has left us an incomparable
formula of this interior proceeding typical of one who
is in search of God: *Fecisti nos ad Te, et inquietum est
cor nostrum donec requiescat in Te.*

4. I do not doubt, dear friends, dear students, men
and women, that I meet your deep convictions here,
evoking in this way the reasons for your presence, but
I am happy to point out the irreplaceable specific role
of your institute and, addressing you, I am thinking
also of the Catholic Universities of France, represented by their rectors, and of similiar institutes.
Their specific task is to initiate into intellectual
research while at the same time meeting your thirst
for certainty and truth. They enable you to unify ex-
istentially, in your intellectual work, two orders of
realities that people too often tend to oppose to each
other as if they were antithetical, the search for truth
and the certainty of already knowing the source of
truth.

This sketch, though too rapid, will be enough to stress the importance I attach to Catholic education in general at its different levels, and in particular to Catholic university thought today. The Catholic atmosphere you desire goes far beyond a mere environment. It includes the desire to be formed to a Christian view of the world, a way of apprehending reality and also of conceiving your studies, however different they may be. I am speaking here, as you well understand, of a perspective which goes beyond the limits and methods of particular sciences to reach the understanding you must have of yourselves, of your role in society, of the meaning of your life.

5. In your university community as a whole, specialized philosophical and theological studies have the first place. It is natural that they should be the heart of the institute. It is natural and also necessary that these sections should be distinguished by the seriousness of their work, their researches and their publications. How glad I am to see that theological teaching is addressed also to lay students in ever larger numbers, offering them the possibility of a Christian formation equal to their culture and professional responsibilities! For what do you seek here, dear friends, but the truth of faith? It is this truth that inspires love of the Church, to which the Lord entrusted it: it is this truth also which requires, by virtue of its internal existence, convinced and faithful adherence to the Magisterium, which alone has been entrusted with the task of interpreting the word of God written and transmitted (cf. *Dei Verbum,* no. 10) and of defining the Faith in conformity with this Revelation (cf. *Lumen gentium,* no. 25). All theological work is in the service of the Faith, I know

that it is a particularly demanding and meritorious service when it is carried out in this way. It has an essential place in the Church, and on its quality depends the Christian authenticity of the researchers themselves, the students and finally the generations to come.

"Let faith think," according to St. Augustine's admirable saying! In Paris, you have long lived in this seething of thought, which can be so creative, as St. Thomas so brilliantly showed in your ancient university, where he was a model student before becoming a model professor. Today as in his time, it is in the same faithfulness that it is necessary to construct anew, but always taking as a basis the Gospel, inexhaustible in its eternal newness, and the doctrine that the Church has clearly formulated.

6. Such is the pastoral commitment of the Catholic Institute. I am thinking in the first place of the laity who benefit from its teaching. I am happy to see them so numerous, so varied. I find again among you a little of Africa, which is even dearer to me now; and Latin America, so well represented here, to which I will go soon. I cannot enumerate all your countries, but I greet you all affectionately. Dear friends, I hope that your studies at the Catholic Institute will enable you to form a deeply Christian and ecclesial conscience.

I am happy to see that the life of prayer flourishes here. Is it not, as it were, the spontaneous blooming of the knowledge of the Lord? May it, by His grace, be strengthened more and more. You cannot progress in it, however, without the question being raised one day, in its widest sense: "How shall I live for Christ?" A question inseparable from the personal consciousness of the requirements of a true Christian life. Such a question matures slowly and develops its vital force only gradually. It is this question that contributes powerfully to direct your family and professional life, according to your Christian convictions strengthened by the time you spent here. I, too, pray for all you men and women who are listening to me, at the essential moment when you give your life its interior orientation, that you may be able to accept this question if it becomes more urgent, more immediate: "What must I do for the Lord?" May He inspire the answer in you Himself!

Saying this to you, I have already approached the consideration of your responsibilities. As the first beneficiaries of the formation you receive, you cannot ignore what it commits you to. Most Reverend d'Hulst, the founder of the Catholic Institute over a century ago now, said that it had been established "to cast a Christian ferment in the thinking world." That creates obligations for you, for today and for tomorrow, in your various countries and also beyond.

7. I have just referred to the Lord's call. I now turn to the priests, seminarians, men and women religious who are continuing their formation here. Rest assured that you have a great place in my heart and in my prayer. Prepare ardently for the task of evangelization that awaits you. In France, the Church has long been a missionary Church, anticipating in this way the orientations of the Second Vatican Council. Without going back further, this missionary activity would amply suffice for the glory of the last century, a magnificent century in which the dynamism of faith, far from letting itself be disheartened by the immensity of the task, blossomed in a host of Christian families, priestly and religious vocations, institutions of every kind that have

gone far beyond the frontiers of France. During the days I spent in the Churches of Africa, so much alive, I was the admiring witness of the harvests that are ripening, the fruit of the obscure and persevering work to which so many missionaries sacrificed their lives. The Catholic Institute was founded in this period. According to its specific vocation, it took its part in this work. Today, more than ever, the harvest is plentiful! You are preparing here to enter the field of the Master of the harvest. Tomorrow, in France, as in your respective countries: you know how much the Church counts on you.

8. I said that I was addressing the students particularly. But now, I wish to turn also to all those who are dedicated to their service here, because they have realized the importance of this ecclesial task and have in many cases dedicated most of their lives to it: in the first place the teaching staff as a whole which is particularly numerous and competent, to deal with the many specializations; the administrators of the Catholic Institute and all those who enable it to live. I am happy to express deep gratitude to them.

9. Ladies and gentlemen, dear friends, men and women students, concluding this too short visit, I say to you: be faithful to the heritage received. Continue to be sensitive to the appeals that reach you. Do not let yourselves be suffocated by the weight of secularization, reject the ferment of doubt, the suspicion of the human sciences, the encroaching practical materialism.... In this historic place, I wish to call you to share my hope and to tell you of my trust. Here, the disciples of St. Teresa and St. John of the Cross have left you the memory and the example of a life entirely consecrated to contemplation of the one Truth. Here,

priests who came from very different horizons, among whom some of your predecessors in the University of that time, have given the testimony of complete faithfulness. Here, a new stage opened, just over a century ago, with the foundation of the Catholic Institute.

May the Holy Spirit, the Spirit of Pentecost, help you to clarify what is ambiguous, to give warmth to what is indifferent, to enlighten what is obscure, to be before the world true and generous witnesses of Christ's love, for "no one can live without love."

I express the most fervent wishes for your teaching, for your studies, and for your future. I pray to the Lord, with all my heart, to give you His light and to bless you.

THE STORY
OF SALVATION
BEGINS ANEW
WITH EVERY PERSON

After his visit to the Catholic Institute on Trinity Sunday morning, June 1, the Holy Father then went by helicopter to Le Bourget Airport where he concelebrated Mass. Despite the very bad weather, an estimated 350,000 people were present. After the Gospel, His Holiness preached the following homily.

I will begin with my heartfelt thanks to all those who have made a point of gathering here this morning, coming even from the distant provinces of France. To all, my fervent good wishes, and in particular to mothers of families, on this day, the feast of mothers. I now invite you to meditate with me.

1. The words we have just heard have a twofold meaning: they end the Gospel as the time of the revelation of Christ, and at the same time they open it towards the future as the time of the Church, that of an incessant duty and a mission.

Christ said: Go!

He indicates the direction of the way: all nations.

He specifies the task: Teach them, baptize them.

The Church remembers these words on this solemn day, when she wishes particularly to worship God in the interior mystery of the life of the Divinity: God as Father, Son and Holy Spirit.

May these words constitute the essential foundation of our meditation, while we are all, through an admirable disposition of Providence, close to Paris, which is the capital of France, one of the capitals of Europe, one among many others, certainly, but unique in its kind, and one of the capitals of the world.

In the last sentence that the Gospel reports, Christ said: "Go into all the world" (Mk. 16:15).

Today I am with you, dear brothers and sisters, in one of these places from which one can see "the world" in a special way, one can see the history of our "world" and one can see the modern "world," the place from where this world knows itself and judges itself, knows and judges its victories and its defeats, its sufferings and its hopes.

Allow me to let myself be carried away, with you, by the extraordinary eloquence of the words that Christ addressed to His disciples. Allow us, through them, to fix our eyes, at least for a moment, on the unfathomable mystery of God, and to touch what, in man, is lasting and consequently most human.

Allow us to prepare in this way for the celebration of the Eucharist, on the feast of the Holy Trinity.

LINK WITH POLAND

2. Christ said to the Apostles: "Go..., make disciples of all nations...." Just as today I find myself practically in the capital of France, so, a year ago, on this same day, the first Sunday after Pentecost, I found myself in a large meadow of the ancient capital of Poland, Krakow, in the city where I lived and from where Christ called me to the Roman See of the apos-

In the last sentence that the Gospel reports, Christ said: "Go into all the world" (Mk. 16:15).

Today I am with you, dear brothers and sisters, in one of these places from which one can see "the world" in a special way, one can see the history of our "world" and one can see the modern "world," the place from where this world knows itself and judges itself, knows and judges its victories and its defeats, its sufferings and its hopes.

tle Peter. There I had before my eyes the well-known faces of my fellow countrymen, and I had before my eyes the whole history of my nation, from its baptism. This rich and difficult history had started, in an admirable way, almost exactly at the moment when Christ's last words to the Apostles: "Make disciples of all the nations, baptize them," were fulfilled. With baptism the nation was born, and its history started.

This nation—the nation whose son I am—is not unknown to you. In the most difficult periods of its history, particularly, it found among you the support it needed, the main architects of its culture, the spokesmen of its independence. I cannot but remember this now. I speak of it with gratitude....

Far later than in France, the missionary paths of the successors of the Apostles reached the Vistula, the Carpathians, the Baltic Sea.... Here, in France, the mission given by Christ to the Apostles after the Resurrection was very soon started, if not with certainty in the apostolic era, at least from the second century, with Irenaeus, the great martyr and apostolic father, who was Bishop of Lyons. Mention of *Lutetia Parisiorum* is very often made, moreover, in the Roman Martyrology....

First Gaul, and then France: the eldest daughter of the Church!

Today, in the capital of the history of your nation, I would like to repeat these words—the title on which you pride yourselves—eldest daughter of the Church.

I would like, taking up this title again, to worship with you the admirable mystery of Providence. I would like to pay homage to the living God who, acting through the peoples, writes the history of salvation in man's heart.

This history is as old as man. It goes back even to his "prehistory"; it goes back to the beginning. When Christ said to the Apostles: "Go, make disciples of all the nations,..." He already confirmed the duration of the history of salvation, and at the same time He proclaimed this particular stage, the last one.

SAINTS OF FRANCE

3. This particular history is hidden in the inmost recesses of man, it is mysterious and yet real too in its historical reality; it is clad, visibly, in facts, events, human existences, individualities. A very great chapter of this history was inscribed in the history of your country, by the sons and daughters of your nation. It would be difficult to name them all, but I will recall at least those who exercised the greatest influence on my life: Joan of Arc, Francis de Sales, Vincent de Paul, Louis-Mary Grignon de Montfort, John-Mary Vianney, Bernadette of Lourdes, Thérèse of Lisieux, Sister Elizabeth of the Trinity, Father de Foucauld, and all the others. They are so present in the life of the whole Church, so influential through the light and the power of the Holy Spirit!

They would all tell you better than I that the history of salvation began with the history of man, that the history of salvation is always beginning anew, that it begins in every man coming into this world. In this way, the history of salvation enters the history of peoples, nations, countries and continents.

The history of salvation begins in God. This is precisely what Christ revealed and declared up to the end when He said: "Go...make disciples of all nations, baptizing them in the name of the Father and of the Son and of the Holy Spirit."

"To baptize" means "to plunge," and the quote "name" means the very reality that it expresses. To baptize in the name of the Father and of the Son and of the Holy Spirit means plunging man into this very Reality that we express by the name of Father, Son and Holy Spirit, the Reality that God is in His divinity: the quite unfathomable Reality, which is completely recognizable and understandable only to itself. At the same time, Baptism plunges man into this Reality which, as Father, Son and Holy Spirit, has opened to man. It has really opened. Nothing is more real than this opening, this communication, this gift to man of the ineffable God. When we hear the names of the Father, the Son and the Holy Spirit, they speak to us precisely of this gift, of this extraordinary "communication" of God who, in Himself, is impenetrable to man.... This communication, this gift, is from the Father, it reached its historical summit and its fullness in the crucified and risen Son, it still remains in the Spirit, who "intercedes for us with sighs too deep for words" (Rom. 8:26).

The words that Christ, at the end of His historical mission, addressed to the Apostles are an absolute synthesis of everything that had constituted this mission, stage by stage from the annunciation to the crucifixion...and finally to the resurrection.

IN GOD'S IMAGE

4. At the heart of this mission, at the heart of the mission of Christ, there is man, every man. Through man, there are the nations, all the nations.

Today's liturgy is theocentric, and yet it is man that it proclaims. It proclaims him because man is at the very heart of the mystery of Christ, man is in the heart of the Father, and of the Son and of the Holy Spirit. And that since the beginning. Was he not created in the image and resemblance of God? Outside that, man is meaningless. Man has a meaning in the world only as the image and likeness of God. Otherwise he has no meaning, and we would end up by saying, as some people have affirmed, that man is only a "useless passion."

Yes. It is man who is proclaimed, he, too, by today's liturgy.

"When I look at your heavens, the work of your
    fingers,
the moon and the stars which you have estab-
    lished;
what is man that you are mindful of him,
and the son of man that you care for him?
Yet you have made him a little less than the
    angels,
and have crowned him with glory and honor.
You have given him *domination over the works* of
    your hands,
you have put all things under his feet" (Ps. 8:3-7).

AFFIRMATION OF MAN

5. Man...praise of man...the affirmation of man.

Yes, the affirmation of the entire man, in his spiritual and corporal constitution, in what manifests him as a subject exteriorly and interiorly. Man adapted, in his visible structure, to all the creatures of the visible world, and at the same time interiorly allied with eternal wisdom.

This wisdom, too, is proclaimed by today's liturgy, which sings of its divine origin, its perceptible presence in the whole work of creation, and ends up by saying that it "delights in the sons of men" (cf. Prv. 8:31).

What have the sons and daughters of your nation not done for the knowledge of man, to express man through the formulation of his inalienable rights! Everyone knows the place that the idea of freedom, equality and brotherhood has in your culture, in your history. Fundamentally, they are Christian ideas. I say so though I am quite aware that those who were the first to formulate this ideal in this way were not referring to man's covenant with eternal wisdom. But they wished to act for man.

For us, the interior covenant with wisdom is the foundation of all culture and of man's real progress.

Are modern development and the progress in which we take part the fruit of the covenant with wisdom? Are they not just an increasingly exact science of objects and things, on which the vertiginous progress of technology is constructed? Is not man, the architect of this progress, becoming more and more the object of this process? And lo, in him and around him this covenant with wisdom is collapsing more and more, the eternal covenant with wisdom which is itself the source of culture, that is, of man's real growth.

WITH ETERNAL WISDOM

6. Christ came into the world in the name of man's covenant with eternal wisdom. In the name of this covenant, He was born of the Virgin Mary, and He

proclaimed the Gospel. In the name of this covenant, "crucified...under Pontius Pilate," He was crucified, and He rose again. In the name of this covenant, renewed in His death and His resurrection, He gives us His Spirit....

The covenant with eternal wisdom continues in Him. It continues in the name of the Father, and of the Son and of the Holy Spirit. It continues as the fact of teaching the nations and baptizing, as the Gospel and the Eucharist. It continues as the Church, that is, the Body of Christ, the People of God.

In this covenant, man must grow and develop as a man. He must grow and develop on the basis of the divine foundation of his humanity, that is, as the image and likeness of God Himself. He must grow and develop as a son of divine adoption.

As a son of divine adoption, man must grow and develop through everything that contributes to the development and progress of the world in which he lives. Through all the works of his hands and his genius. Through the success of contemporary science and the application of modern technology. Through everything he knows about the macrocosm and the microcosm, thanks to a more and more perfected equipment.

How does it come about that, for some time now, man has discovered in all this gigantic progress a source of menace for himself? How and by what ways have we reached the point that, at the very heart of modern science and technology, there has appeared the possibility of the gigantic self-destruction of man; that daily life offers so many proofs of the use, against man, of what should be for man and should serve man?

How have we reached this point? Has not man on his way to progress taken only one way, the easier one, and has he not neglected the alliance with eternal wisdom? Has he not taken the "wide" way, neglecting the "narrow" way? (cf. Mt. 7:13-14)

MEANING OF AUTHORITY

7. Christ says: "All authority in heaven and on earth has been given to me" (Mt. 28:18). He says so when earthly power—the Sanhedrin, the power of Pilate—has shown its supremacy over him, by decreeing His death on the cross. He says so also after His resurrection.

"Authority in heaven and on earth" is not an authority against man. It is not even an authority of man over man. It is the authority that enables man to be revealed to himself in his royalty, in all the fullness of his dignity. It is the authority the specific power of which man must discover in his heart, through which he must be revealed to himself in the dimensions of his conscience and in the perspective of eternal life. Then the whole power of baptism will be revealed in him, he will know that he is "plunged" in the Father, the Son and the Holy Spirit; he will find himself again completely in the eternal Word, in infinite Love.

That is what man is called to in the covenant with eternal wisdom.

Such, too, is this "authority" that Christ has "in heaven and on earth."

The man of today has greatly increased his power over the earth; he is even thinking of his expansion beyond our planet.

It can be said at the same time that man's power over the other man is becoming heavier and heavier.

Abandoning the covenant with eternal wisdom, he is less and less able to govern himself, nor is he able to govern others. How pressing the question of fundamental human rights has become! What a threatening face totalitarianism and imperialism reveal! In them man ceases to be the subject, which is tantamount to saying that he ceases to count as a man. He counts only as a unity and an object!

Let us listen once more to what Christ said through these words: "All authority in heaven and on earth has been given to me," and let us meditate on the whole truth of these words.

8. Christ, at the end, says further: "I am with you always, to the close of the age" (Mt. 28:20); so that also means: today, in 1980, for the whole of our era.

The problem of the absence of Christ does not exist. The problem of His moving away from man's history does not exist. God's silence with regard to the anxieties of man's heart and his fate does not exist.

There is only one problem that exists always and everywhere: the problem of our presence beside Christ. Of our remaining in Christ. Of our intimacy with the authentic truth of His words and with the power of His love. There exists only one problem, that of our faithfulness to the covenant with eternal wisdom, which is the source of true culture, that is, of man's growth, and that of faithfulness to the promises of our baptism in the name of the Father, and of the Son and of the Holy Spirit!

Then allow me, in conclusion, to question you:
France, eldest Daughter of the Church, are you faithful to the promises of your baptism?

Allow me to ask you:

France, Daughter of the Church and educator of peoples, are you faithful, for the good of man, to the covenant with eternal wisdom?

Forgive me this question. I asked it as the minister does at the moment of baptism. I asked it out of solicitude for the Church whose first priest and first servant I am, and out of love for man, whose definitive greatness is in God, Father, Son and Holy Spirit.

MAY MARY WATCH OVER FRANCE

Before the conclusion of the Holy Mass that the Pope con-celebrated on Sunday, June 1, at the airport of Le Bourget, John Paul II delivered the following address before the recitation of the Angelus.

Dear brothers and sisters,

Today, in every family of France, the mother will be honored and fêted. The children will offer her the best gift that their heart has chosen. It is a beautiful thing that everyone should turn especially towards his mother, when he has the good fortune to have her still, for it is she who introduces man to life, it is she who teaches him to love by being the first to surround him with affection.

Likewise, we Christians must often turn towards Mary, for through her, thanks to the Holy Spirit, we received Christ who made us acquainted with the tenderness of our Father in heaven. How could we live our baptism, without contemplating Mary, blessed among all women, so ready to receive God's gift? Christ gave her to us as a Mother. He gave her to the Church as a Mother. She shows us the way. What is more, she intercedes for us. Spontaneously every Catholic entrusts his prayer to her, and even dedicates himself to her in order to dedicate himself better to God.

You know very well this beautiful custom of the Church of marking the morning, midday and the evening with a pause for prayer, the Angelus, in order to repeat to Mary the first greeting of the Angel Gabriel and her own answer, to enter, ourselves, the mystery of God made man. The bells of your churches often continue to invite you to this prayer, which we are going to say together. May Mary watch over each of your families, over each of your cities! May she watch over France!

FOR A SOCIETY FREE OF DISCRIMINATIONS

In the afternoon of Sunday, June 1, the Holy Father, on his arrival at the Seminary of Issy les Moulineaux, met the Chief Rabbi of France, Jacob Kaplan, and some leaders of the Jewish community. During the meeting, Pope John Paul II delivered the following address.

Dear brothers,

It is a joy for me to receive the representatives of the numerous and vigorous Jewish community of France. This community has, indeed, a long and glorious history. Is it necessary to recall here the theologians, exegetes, philosophers and personages of public life who have distinguished it in the past and still distinguish it? It is true also, and I make a point of mentioning it, that your community suffered a great deal during the dark years of the occupation and the war. I pay homage to these victims, whose sacrifice, we know, has not been fruitless. It was from there that there really began, thanks to the courage and decision of some pioneers, including Jules Isaac, the movement that has led us to the present dialogue and collaboration, inspired and promoted by the Declaration *Nostra aetate* of the Second Vatican Council.

This dialogue and this collaboration are very much alive and active here in France. This makes me happy. Between Judaism and the Church, there is a relationship, as I said on another occasion to Jewish representatives, a relationship "at the very level of their respective religious identities'' (Address of March 12, 1979). This relationship must be further deepened and enriched by study, mutual knowledge, religious education on both sides, and the effort to overcome the difficulties that still exist. That will enable us to work together for a society free of discriminations and prejudices, in which love and not hatred, peace and not war, justice and not oppression, may reign. It is towards this biblical ideal that we should always look, since it unites us so deeply. I take advantage of this happy opportunity to reaffirm it to you again and to express to you my hope of pursuing it together.

DISCERNMENT BETWEEN RENEWAL AND MODERN SECULARIZATION

On Sunday afternoon, June 1, John Paul II traveled by helicopter to the Seminary of Issy les Moulineaux. After meeting a Jewish delegation, he went to the seminary chapel where he met the French bishops, who were meeting in extraordinary plenary assembly, and addressed them as follows.

1. God be praised for having given us time for quite a long meeting in the framework of this short visit! I attach great importance to this meeting for reasons of "collegiality." We know that collegiality has a twofold character: it is "effective," but it is also "affective." And that is deeply in conformity with its origin around Christ in the communion of the "Twelve."

We are living, therefore, an important moment of our episcopal communion, the Bishops of France around the Bishop of Rome who, this time, is their guest, whereas he has received them on various occasions other times, for example in the course of the *ad limina* visits, especially in 1977 when Paul VI surveyed with you a large number of questions, in a way that is still very valid today. We must thank God that Vatican II undertook, confirmed and renewed the doctrine on the collegiality of the episcopate, as the living and authentic expression of the college which, by the institution of Christ, the Apostles constituted with Peter at their head. We give thanks to God also for our being able, along this way, to carry out our mission better: to bear witness to the Gospel, and to serve the Church and also the modern world, to which we have been sent together with the whole Church.

I thank you heartily for having invited me, for having finalized, with great care, the details of this pastoral visit, for having carried out so many preparations, for having explained to the Christian people the meaning of my coming, for having shown eagerness and openness which are such important attitudes for our mission as pastors and teachers of the Faith. I pay tribute especially to Cardinal Marty who receives us in the seminary of his province; to Cardinal Etchegaray, President of the Episcopal Conference; to Cardinal Renard, the Primate of the Gauls; to Cardinal Gouyon and to Cardinal Guyot; but it would be necessary for me to name each bishop, and that is not possible. I have had the honor to meet and collaborate with a certain number of you in the past: first of all in the sessions of the Council, of course, but also in the various synods, at the Council of the Episcopal Conferences of Europe, or on other occasions, of which I preserve a happy memory. That enables us to work easily together, even if I now come with a special responsibility.

ESCHATOLOGICAL YET FULLY HISTORICAL

2. The mission of the Church, which is continually realized in the eschatological perspective, is at the same time fully historical. That is connected with the duty of reading "the signs of the times," which was so deeply considered by Vatican II. With great perspicacity, the Council also defined what the mission of the Church is in the present stage of history. Our common task remains, therefore, the acceptance and implementation of Vatican II, according to its authentic content. Doing so, we are guided by faith: it is our main and fundamental reason for acting. We believe that Christ, through the Holy Spirit, was with the Conciliar Fathers, that the Council contains, in its Magisterium, what the Spirit "says to the Church," and that He says it at the same time in full harmony with tradition and according to the requirements dictated by the "signs of the times." This faith is based on Christ's promise: "I am with you always, to the close of the age" (Mt 28:20). On this faith is founded also our conviction that we must "implement the Council" such as it is, and not as some people would like to see and understand it.

There is nothing surprising about the fact that, in this "post-conciliar" stage, there have also developed, quite intensely, certain interpretations of Vatican II which do not correspond to its authentic Magisterium. It is a question here of two well-known trends: "progressivism" and "integralism." The first are always eager to adapt even the content of faith, Christian ethics, the liturgy, ecclesial organization, to changes of mentalities, and to the demands of the "world," without sufficiently taking into account not only the general feeling of the faithful, who are bewildered, but also the essentials of the faith, already defined, the roots of the Church, her centuries-old experience, the norms necessary for her faithfulness, her unity, her universality. They are obsessed about "advancing," but towards what "progress," when all is said and done? The others—pointing out these abuses which we are, of course, the first to condemn and correct—adopt an intransient attitude, shutting themselves up in a given period of the Church, at a given stage of theological formulation of liturgical expression which they make an absolute, without sufficiently penetrating its underlying meaning, without considering the totality of history and its legitimate development, fearing new questions, without admitting, in a word, that the Spirit of God is at work in the Church today, with her pastors united with the Successor of Peter.

SIMILAR SITUATIONS

These facts are not surprising if we think of similar phenomena in the history of the Church. But it is all the more necessary to concentrate all forces on the correct, that is, authentic interpretation of the conciliar Magisterium, as the indispensable foundation of the further self-realization of the Church, for which this Magisterium is the source of correct inspirations and orientations. The two extreme trends which I have pointed out foster not only an opposition, but a regrettable and harmful division, as if they stirred up each other to the extent of creating uneasiness for everyone, even scandal, and of expending in this mutual suspicion and criticism so many energies which would be so useful for a real renewal. It is to be hoped that both parties, which do not lack generosity or faith, will learn humbly, with their pastors, to overcome this opposition between brothers, to accept the authentic interpretation of the Council—for that is the fundamental question—and to face up together to the mission of the Church, in the diversity of their pastoral sensitivity.

Certainly, the vast majority of Christians in your country are ready to manifest their faithfulness and their readiness to follow the Church; they do not share these extreme and unauthorized positions, but a certain number hesitate between the two or are troubled by them; and the problem is also that they run the risk of becoming indifferent and of straying from the Faith. The time makes it necessary for you to be more than ever the architects of unity, watching over the fundamental questions which are at stake and at the same time the psychological difficulties which prevent ecclesial life in truth and in charity.

MODERN MAN TEMPTED TO DENY GOD

3. I now come to another fundamental question: why is a particular concentration on man necessary, in the present stage of the mission of the Church? I developed that in the encyclical *Redemptor hominis,* trying to highlight the fact that this anthropological emphasis has a deep and strong Christological root.

The causes vary. There are visible and perceptible causes, according to the multiple variations which depend, for example, on the environment, the country, the nation, history and culture. There certainly exists, therefore, a specific set of causes which

are characteristic of the "French" reality of the
Church in the modern world. You are in the best position to know them and understand them. If I take the
liberty of tackling this subject, I do so with the conviction that the problem—in view of the present state of
civilization on the one hand and the threats which
weigh on humanity on the other hand—has a dimension that is at once fundamental and universal. In this
universal and at the same time local dimension, the
Church must consequently face up to the common
problems of man as an integral part of her evangelical
mission.

Not only is the Gospel message addressed to man,
but it is a great Messianic message about man: it is the
revelation to man of the complete truth about himself
and about his vocation in Christ (cf. *Gaudium et spes*).

Proclaiming this message, we are at the center of
the implementation of Vatican II. The application of
this message is imposed on us, moreover, by the overall situation of man in the modern world. I would not
like to repeat what has already been said in *Gaudium
et spes* and in *Redemptor hominis,* to which reference
must always be made. However, it is perhaps not an
exaggeration to say, in this place and in this framework, that we are living in a stage of particular temptation for man.

We know different stages of this temptation,
beginning with the first one, in chapter three of Genesis, up to the highly significant temptations which
Christ Himself underwent. They are, as it were, a
synthesis of all the temptations that arise from the
three forms of lust. The present-day temptation, however, goes further (it could almost be said that it is a
"meta-temptation"); it goes "beyond" everything

that, in the course of history, has constituted the subject of the temptation of man, and it manifests at the
same time, it could be said, the very substance of all
temptations. Modern man undergoes the temptation
of denying God in the name of his own humanity.

It is a temptation that is particularly deep and particularly threatening from the anthropological point
of view, if it is considered that man has no meaning
himself unless as the image and likeness of God.

MATURE FAITH ANIMATED BY LOVE

4. As pastors of the Church sent to the man of our
time, we must be clearly aware of this temptation, in
its multiple aspects, not for the purpose of "judging
man," but to love him even more: "to love" always
means in the first place "to understand."

Together with this attitude which we would call a
passive one, we must have, equally deeply, a positive
attitude, I mean awareness of the fact that historical
man is very deeply inscribed in the mystery of Christ,
awareness of the anthropological capacity of this mystery, of "the breadth and length and height and
depth," according to St. Paul's expression (Eph. 3:18).

We must then be particularly ready for dialogue.
But first of all its main meaning and its fundamental
conditions must be defined.

According to the thought of Paul VI, and it can
also be said, of the Council, "dialogue" certainly
means openness, the capacity of understanding another down to his very roots: his history, the path he
has traversed, the inspirations that animate him. It
does not mean either indifferentism, or in any way
"the art of confusing essential concepts"; now, unfor-

tunately, this art is very often recognized as equivalent to the attitude of "dialogue." Nor does it mean "veiling" the truth of one's convictions, of one's "credo."

Certainly, the Council requires from the Church in our age a faith open to dialogue in the different circles of interlocutors of whom Paul VI spoke; it also requires that her faith should be capable of recognizing all the seeds of truth wherever they may be. But, for this very reason, it requires from the Church a very mature faith, a faith highly conscious of its own truth, and at the same time very deeply animated by love.

All that is important by reason of our mission as pastors of the Church and as preachers of the Gospel.

The fact must also be taken into consideration that these modern forms of the temptation of man taking man as an absolute, also reach the community of the Church, also become forms of her temptation, and endeavor in this way to turn her aside from the self-realization to which she was called by the Spirit of Truth, precisely by the Council of our century.

On the one hand, we find ourselves up against the threat of "systematic" atheization, "enforced" in a way in the name of man's progress; but on the other hand, there is here another threat, within the Church: it consists of wishing, in many ways, "to conform to the world" in its present "advanced" aspect.

We know how much this desire is radically distinguished from what Christ taught. It is enough to recall the Gospel comparison of the leaven and that of the salt of the earth, to warn the Apostles against conformity with the world.

Nevertheless there is no lack of pioneers or "prophets" of this direction of "progress" in the Church.

GREAT TASK TO PRESERVE
THE DEPOSIT OF FAITH

5. This shows the vastness of the task of pastors as regards "discernment," between what is a real "renewal" and what is a cover for the trends of modern "secularization" and "laicization," or else the tendency towards "compromise" with a system without knowing, perhaps, all its premises.

It also shows how great is the task of pastors to "preserve the deposit," to remain faithful to the mystery of Christ inscribed in the whole of man's history, and also to remain faithful to this marvelous "supernatural sense of faith" of the whole People of God, which is generally not the object of publicity in the mass media, but which is expressed in the depth of hearts and consciences with the authentic language of the Spirit. Our doctrinal and pastoral ministry must remain particularly in the service of this *"sensus fidelium,"* as the Constitution *Lumen gentium* (no. 12) recalled.

At a time when people talk so much of "prophetic charism"—not always using this concept in accordance with its exact meaning—it is necessary to renew deeply and reconstruct the awareness of prophetic charism linked with the episcopal ministry of the teachers of faith and "guides of the flock," who incarnate in life, according to an adequate analogy, Christ's words about the "Good Shepherd."

The Good Shepherd is concerned about pasturage, about feeding His sheep. Here, I am thinking particularly of the theological publications, which spread very quickly and far and wide, and in many environments, and of which the essential parts are popularized in reviews. It is they which, according to their qualities, their depth, their sense of the Church, educate and deepen faith, or on the contrary shake it or dissolve it through their partiality or their methods. French publications have often had, and still have, an international readership, even among the young Churches. Your prophetic charism makes it a duty for you to watch particularly over their doctrinal faithfulness, and their ecclesial quality.

EFFORTS OF THE CHURCH IN FRANCE

6. The fundamental question that we must ask ourselves, we bishops on whom there weighs a special responsibility as regards the truth of the Gospel and the mission of the Church, is that of the credibility of this mission and of our service. In this field, we are sometimes questioned and judged severely; did not one of you write: "Our age will have been harsh with regard to the bishops"? Then, too, we are ready to judge ourselves severely, and to judge severely the religious situation of the country and the results of our apostolate. The Church in France has not been free from such judgments: it is enough to recall the famous book of Abbé Godin, *France, pays de mission?* (France, a mission country?), or else the well-known statement: "The Church has lost the working class."

These judgments sometimes call for a perspicacious moderation to be observed. It is also necessary to think for the long term, for that is essential for our mission. But it cannot be denied that the Church in France has undertaken, and is undertaking, great efforts in order "to reach those who are far away," especially in the dechristianized working class and rural environments.

These efforts must preserve fully an evangelical, apostolic and pastoral character. It is not possible to succumb to "the challenges of politics." Nor can we accept many resolutions which claim to be only "just." We cannot let ourselves be shut up in overall views which are in reality one-sided. It is true that social mechanisms, and also their political and economic characteristics, seem to confirm these overall views and certain painful facts: "mission country," "loss of the working class." It seems, however, that we must be ready not only for "self-criticism," but also for "criticism" of the mechanisms themselves. The Church must be ready to defend the rights of the workers, in every economic and political system.

Above all, the very great contribution of the Church and of French Catholicism in the missionary field of the Church, for example, or the field of Christian culture, cannot be forgotten. It cannot be accepted that these chapters should be closed! What is more, it cannot be accepted that, in these fields, the Church in France should change the quality of its contribution and the orientation it had taken, which merits complete credibility.

It would, of course, be necessary to consider here a whole series of elementary tasks within the Church, in France itself, for example catechesis, the apostolate of the family, the work of vocations, seminaries, Catholic education, theology. All that in a great synthesis of this "credibility" which is so necessary for the Church in France, as everywhere, and for the common good of the universal Church.

A really universal view of the Church and of the world is necessary, and a particularly precise one, I would say "without an error." You cannot act only according to circumstances that presented themselves to you in the past and that are still offered to you. You must have a precise and exact "plan of solidarity," with regard to those who have a special right to rely on your solidarity and expect it from you.... A particular solidarity of witness and common prayer is necessary!

THE SENSE
OF SELF-SACRIFICE

7. Your responsibility extends in fact—as among other episcopates, but in a different way—beyond "your" Church, beyond France. This is something you must accept and you cannot shake it off. There again, a really universal view of the Church and of the world is necessary, and a particularly precise one, I would say "without an error." You cannot act only according to circumstances that presented themselves to you in the past and that are still offered to you. You must have a precise and exact "plan of solidarity," with regard to those who have a special right to rely on your solidarity and expect it from you. You must have your eyes wide open to the West and to the East, to the North and to the South. You must bear witness to your solidarity with those who are suffering from hunger and injustice, owing to the heritage of colonialism or the defective distribution of material goods. But you must also be very sensitive to all the harm that is being done to the human spirit: to conscience, religious convictions, etc. Do not forget that the future of the Gospel and of the Church is being worked out, perhaps, particularly where men sometimes undergo, for their Faith and for the consequences of faith, sacrifices worthy of the early Christians. You cannot remain silent about that before your society and your Church. In this field a particular solidarity of witness and common prayer is necessary!

That is a sure way of strengthening the credibility of the Church in your country, and it must not be abandoned. You have your place, in fact, in a system of communicating vessels, even if, in this system, you are unquestionably a particularly venerable, particularly important and influential element. That creates a great many duties! The way to the future of the Church in France—the way perhaps to the great conversion, the need of which is felt by bishops, priests and faithful—passes through the acceptance of these duties!

But in face of the denials which concern many people, in face of the despair which, following upon the numerous vicissitudes of history, seems to form the spiritual face of modern society, do you not still have the same powerful structure of the Gospel and of holiness, which is a special heritage of the Church in France?

Does not Christianity belong immanently to the "genius of your nation"?

Is not France still "the eldest Daughter of the Church"?

GENEROUSLY AVAILABLE FOR THE CHURCH'S NEEDS

On Sunday afternoon, June 1, after his address to the French bishops, the Holy Father went to the auditorium of the seminary at Issy les Moulineaux where he met the 220 seminarians and numerous members of the priests' councils of the Paris region. He spoke to them as follows.

Dear seminarian friends,

1. I could not conclude this afternoon without spending a moment with you, getting to know your faces, and exhorting you in the name of the Lord. What joy to meet you, you young students in formation in the Paris region! I have been told that there are gathered here the students of the St. Sulpice Seminary, those of the University Seminary of the Carmelites and members of different preparatory groups. Fine. I am happy that it is possible to count on your availability to serve, on your generosity. Addressing these few words to you, you will allow me to address at the same time all your French confreres who, elsewhere in this country, but also in my diocese of Rome, are following the same way.

As you know, I have just had a long working-session with your bishops. It was a particularly important conversation, in the course of which we were able, we who are jointly in charge of all the Churches, to face up to our responsibilities in order to assume them according to what pleases God. And now, it seems quite natural to continue this conversation, in a way, with those who are preparing to become collaborators of the episcopal order, and to be associated in this way, in the person of Christ, with the preaching of the Gospel and the guidance of the People of God. You are still young, certainly, but already you divine a great many things. You understand that your gift must be complete and that, the further you go, the more you will discover the necessity of making it— if I may venture to say so—even more complete. It is at this level, therefore, that I will take up my position with you, taking into account, of course, the fact that a way such as yours takes time, and a long spiritual, intellectual and pastoral maturation, and that the mere desire to become a priest is not enough in itself to meet the requirements of the priesthood.

DISCOVER THE SENSE
OF SELF-SACRIFICE

2. One of these requirements, the most fundamental one is that you should be deeply rooted in Jesus Christ. I invite you to this with all my heart. If you could learn, through prayer and contemplation, to live, preach, love and suffer like Christ, it seems that the main lines of your mission would gradually take shape clearly, and that you would also feel a vital need to join men and bring them what they really need. In such a proceeding there is already the soul of the apostolate, so that "action" is indissolubly linked

with "being," and vice versa. Here it is not useful to pursue vain discussions, nor is it good to prefer one to the detriment of the other. The Church intends to form you in complete interior unity, in which the mission requires intimacy with God, and in which the latter calls for the former.

Do you not want to be, yourselves, "good shepherds"? The good shepherd gives his life, and he gives his life for his sheep. Very well, then! It is necessary to discover the sense of self-sacrifice, linked with the sacrifice of Christ, and offer yourselves for others, who expect this witness from you. That can be said of all the faithful, but with all the more reason and in a very special way of priests and future priests. May your daily participation in the Eucharist and the efforts you make to increase Eucharistic devotion within you, help you along this way!

PASTORAL WISDOM

3. I was speaking to you a moment ago of unity among yourselves. In my opinion, it makes it possible to acquire what could be called pastoral wisdom. One of the fruits of the conciliar decree of Vatican II on the formation of priests was certainly to create the conditions for better pastoral preparation of candidates. Thanks to the inner balance you achieve, you must be able to improve your judgment of men, things and situations, and view them in the light of God and not with the eyes of the world. That will lead you to a deep perception of the problems, and of the multiple urgent needs of the mission, and at the same time that will urge you on towards the right goal. In this way you will be less exposed to the temptation of "extol-

ling'' only what our contemporaries are living, or on the contrary of experimenting on them pastoral ideas that are perhaps generous, but personal and without the guarantee of the Church: there must be no experimenting on men. You will take to heart, for this very reason, your intellectual work, indispensable today as it is after ordination, in order to transmit to others the whole content of faith in an exact, harmonious synthesis, easy to assimilate.

Is it necessary, besides, to point out that the priest is one among others? By himself, he cannot be everything to everyone. His ministry is exercised within a presbyterium, around a bishop. Such already in a small way is your own case, to the extent that your bonds with your diocese, where you are integrated in the pastoral teams to develop in you the capacity of working as a Church, are gradually strengthened. And if your personal path—or the stress sometimes laid on such and such an aspect of your preparation—make you more suitable for a given type of ministry, among a more particular category of the population, nevertheless you will be sent basically to everyone, with pastoral concern for everyone and the determination to collaborate with everyone, excluding no trend or environment. You must be capable also of accepting any ministry that is entrusted to you, without subordinating your acceptance to conformity with expediency or personal projects. In this matter, it is the needs of the Church that have priority, and it is necessary to adapt oneself to them. This seems absolutely essential to your bishops and myself, in consideration of the office with which Providence has invested us and with which you will be associated one day.

WITH FAITH AND JOY

4. My dear sons, you see the vastness of the task, the vastness of the needs. You are not very numerous, and yet the efforts undertaken for several years are beginning to yield visible results. I shall not tell you that the generosity of the laity will make it possible to mitigate the lack of priests. It is completely of another order. In the laity you will always have to develop the sense of responsibility and to educate them to take their full place in the community. But what God has put in your hearts through His call corresponds to a specific vocation. Try to bear witness better to your faith and your joy. You are the witnesses of priestly vocations among adolescents and young people of your age. Ah! If you could realize the hope that is in you, and show that the mission cannot wait, in France and even more in other less privileged countries! I encourage you with all my strength to be the first apostles of vocations.

PRIESTS OF QUALITY

5. I also wish to encourage and thank your teachers and educators at all levels: rectors of seminaries, diocesan delegates, parish priests, chaplaincies and movements which contribute to your formation, and those who enabled you to discern the Lord's call. You owe them a great deal. The Church owes them a great deal. In this place, I would like to pay tribute especially to priests of the Society of St. Sulpice, who have won the esteem of everyone in their service of the priesthood.

Your educators have a difficult task. It must be known, in France, that I put my trust in them and give them my brotherly support. They wish to form priests of quality. May they continue their efforts and develop them further, with the help of the texts of the Council, the excellent *Rationes* which have been prepared at the request of the Holy See, and the recent documents published by the Congregation for Catholic Education, which they have, I do not doubt, distributed widely among you and commented upon.

My hearty thanks to you all, dear confreres and dear sons. I shall see you later, at the *Parc des Princes,* with the young people of the Paris region, and I bless you with my deep affection.

THE WHOLE GOSPEL IS A DIALOGUE WITH MAN

*On the evening of Sunday, June 1, the Holy Father met over nine-
ty thousand young Parisians gathered at Parc des Princes, the
largest stadium in the French capital, for a prayer vigil.*

*The address that the Holy Father delivered to the young peo-
ple during the meeting was not the one originally prepared for
the occasion. The reason for this change was explained to the
young people by the Pope himself who, before ending the meeting, said: "Before concluding I must tell you how I prepared this
dialogue, this address-dialogue. I was sent the program and I
was told that I had to speak to the young. So then I prepared a
speech. Later the organizers sent me 'your' program and the
questions you wished to ask the Pope. So it was necessary to
change the address I had prepared and prepare the one you have
just heard. But the 'monologue' address, the message, still remains and I would like to leave it to you so that you can read it
and meditate on it. I think the organizers will willingly distribute
it to you."*

QUESTIONS ADDRESSED TO THE POPE BY THE YOUTH OF PARIS

1. In every country that you visited you wished to
meet the youth. Why?

2. In each country you visited you wished to meet
the rulers. Why? What did you say to them?

"Recognize your dignity, O Christian," the great Pope St. Leo said. And I, his unworthy Successor, I say to you, my Catholic brothers and sisters in France: Recognize your dignity! Be proud of your faith, of the gift of the Spirit that the Father has bestowed on you! I come among you as a poor man, with the unique riches of the faith, a pilgrim of the Gospel. Give the Church and the world the example of your unfailing faithfulness and your missionary zeal.

Christ says, "I am with you always, to the close of the age" (Mt. 28:20).

The problem of the absence of Christ does not exist. The problem of His moving away from man's history does not exist. God's silence with regard to the anxieties of man's heart and his fate, does not exist.

There exists only one problem, that of our faithfulness to the covenant with eternal wisdom, which is the source of true culture, that is, of man's growth, and that of faithfulness to the promises of our baptism in the name of the Father, and of the Son and of the Holy Spirit!

Never can the Church resign herself to lacking priests, holy priests. The more the People of God reaches its maturity, and the more Christian families and Christian laity assume their role in their multiple apostolic commitments, the more they need priests who are fully priests, precisely for the vitality of their Christian life. In another direction, the more the world is dechristianized or lacks maturity in faith, the more it, too, needs priests who are completely dedicated to bearing witness to the fullness of Christ's mystery.

On this land which I have the privilege of visiting today, here, in this city, there have been, and there are, many men and women who have known and who still know today that their whole life has a value and meaning solely and exclusively to the extent to which it is an answer to this question (of Christ): Do you love me? They have given, and give, their answer in a complete and perfect way—a heroic answer—or else in a

common, ordinary way. But in any case they know that their lives, that human life in general, has a value and a meaning to the extent to which it is the answer to this question: Do you love? It is only thanks to this question that life is worth living.

I come here in their footsteps. I visit their earthly country. I commend to their intercession France and Paris, the Church and the world.

The measure of the things and events of the created world is man, but the measure of man is God. Therefore, man must always return to this source, to this one measure, which is God incarnate in Jesus Christ, if he wants to be a man, and if the world is to be human. It is precisely to this fundamental and most important truth that I wish to bear witness with this visit of mine to France. Return to this truth, meditate upon it, and in it you will again find yourselves and others, all the vicissitudes that make up human life as a whole, your concrete life and your tasks in all directions.

You should be deeply rooted in Jesus Christ. I invite you to this with all my heart. If you could learn, through prayer and contemplation, to live, preach, love and suffer like Christ, it seems that the main lines of your mission would gradually take shape clearly, and that you would also feel a vital need to join men and bring them what they really need. In such a proceeding there is already the soul of the apostolate, so that "action" is indissolubly linked with "being," and vice versa.

All love, provided it is authentic, pure and disinterested, bears in itself its own justification. To love gratuitously is an inalienable right of the person, even—and one should say, above all—when the Beloved is God Himself. In the footsteps of contemplatives and mystics of all times, continue to bear witness with power and humility to the transcendent dimension of the human person, created in the likeness of God and called to a life of intimacy with Him.

Those of you who have had the possibility of establishing contacts and making friends with young people of another province, another country, another continent than their own, will understand better, perhaps, and certainly share my faith in youth, because they are everywhere, today as yesterday, the bearers of great hopes for the world and for the Church. Young people of France, convinced Christians or sympathizers with Christianity, I would like us, on this unforgettable evening, to make a climb, all roped together, in the direction of the difficult, and at the same time bracing, peaks of the vocation of man, of Christian man.

Man, indeed, through all the formulas with which he tries to define himself, cannot forget that he, too, is a temple: he is the temple in which the Holy Spirit dwells. For this reason, man raised this temple which has borne witness to him for eight centuries: Notre-Dame.

Here, in this place, in the course of our first meeting, this question had to be asked: "Do you love me?" But it must be asked everywhere and always. This question is put to man by God. And man must continually ask himself this question.

Religious life is a friendship, an intimacy of the mystical order with Christ. Your personal path must be, as it were, an original re-edition of the famous poem of the Song of Solomon. Dear sisters, in the heart-to-heart relationship of prayer, absolutely vital for each of you, as on the occasion of your different apostolic commitments, listen to the Lord murmuring the same call to you: "Follow me." The ardor of your response will keep you in the freshness of your first offering. In this way you will go from faithfulness to faithfulness!

If you ask me consequently: "What must we do in the Church, we above all, the young?" I will reply: learn to know Christ. Constantly. To learn Christ. The unfathomable treasures of wisdom and science are really found in Him....

I ask you also to strengthen your union with the young people of the whole Church and of the world, in the spirit of the certainty that Christ is our Way, the Truth and the Life (cf. Jn. 14:16).

Let us do honor to maternity, because faith in man is expressed in it. The act of faith in man is the fact that his parents give him life. The mother bears him in her womb, and she is ready to suffer all the pains of childbirth; thereby, with all her feminine self, with all her maternal self, she proclaims her faith in man. She bears witness to the value which is in her and transcends her at the same time, to the value constituted by the one who, still unknown, just conceived, fully hidden in his mother's womb, must be born and be manifested to the world as a son of his parents, as a confirmation of their humanity, as a fruit of their love, as a future of the family.

To be a witness to Christ, to bear witness to Him, it is necessary, first, to follow Him. It is necessary to learn to know Him, to place oneself, so to speak, in His school, to penetrate all His mystery. It is a fundamental and central task. If we remain attentive to that, Christ Himself will teach us, through His Spirit, what we have to do, how to behave, in what and how to commit ourselves....

Christ's earthly life was a short one, His public life even shorter. But His life is unique, His personality is unique in the world. He is not only a Brother for us, a Friend, a Man of God. We recognize in Him the only Son of God, who is one with God the Father and whom the Father gave to the world. With the apostle Peter, whose humble Successor I am, I profess: "You are the Christ, the Son of the living God." It is precisely because Christ shares at once the divine nature and our human nature that the offering of His life, in His death and His resurrection, reaches us, the men of today, saves us, purifies us, frees us, elevates us.

People of France, raise your eyes more often towards Jesus Christ! He is the Man who loved most, and most consciously, most voluntarily and most gratuitously! Meditate on Christ's testament: "There is no greater proof of love than to give one's life for those one loves."

3. What do you expect to do for the unity of Christians? How do you see this unity?

4. How does one pray as Pope?

5. You have taken pretty severe measures in regard to some theologians. Why?

6. Two years have passed since your election: at this point, how do you see your ministry?

7. Tell us about your own country. What can we learn from Poland? And what can Poland learn from France?

8. You have been in Latin America and in Africa: how do you view the relations between the Third World and countries such as France?

9. Can the Gospel provide an answer for the problems of today?

10. Before being a Bishop and Pope you were a simple priest. How do you view the priest of today?

11. People frequently speak of a Third World War. What can we young people do to prevent it?

12. We wish to be happy. Is it possible to be so in the present-day world?

13. Speak to us simply about Jesus Christ. Who is Jesus Christ for you?

14. Is it necessary to continue the work of Vatican II?

15. What can the Catholic Church do for peace and justice in the world?

16. The Catholic Church is ruled by men. Will women always have a secondary role?

17. As regards sexuality the Catholic Church always adopts decisions which are rather restrictive. Why? Do you not fear that the youth will gradually become estranged from the Church?

18. How can one be a witness of Christ today?

19. What is the role of the laity, and especially of the young, in the Church?

20. The Church is Western. Can it be really African or Asiatic?

21. If we had not submitted these questions to you, what would you have said to us?

The three questions addressed to the Pope in *Parc des Princes* were: If we had not submitted these questions to you, what would you have said to us?

Speak to us simply about Jesus Christ. Who is Jesus Christ for you?

People frequently speak of a Third World War. What can we young people do to prevent it?

In the course of his address, the Holy Father wished to give a complete reply to all twenty-one questions:

Dear young people of France,

1. I thank you for this meeting which you wished to organize as a kind of dialogue. You wanted to speak to the Pope. And that is very important for two reasons.

The first reason is that this way of acting refers us directly to Christ: in Him, there is continually unfolded a dialogue: God's conversation with man and man's with God.

Christ—you have heard—is the Word, the Word of God. He is the eternal Word. This Word of God, like man, is not the word of a "great monologue," but the *Word* of the "incessant dialogue" which takes place in the Holy Spirit. I know that this sentence is difficult to understand, but I say it all the same, and I leave it to you so that you can meditate on it. Did we not celebrate this morning the mystery of the Holy Trinity?

The second reason is the following: the dialogue corresponds to my personal conviction that, to be the servant of the Word, means "proclaiming" in the sense of "answering." To answer, it is necessary to know the questions. So it is a good thing that you asked them; otherwise, I would have had to guess in order to be able to speak to you, to answer you! (That is your question no. 21.)

I have arrived at this conviction, not only because of my experience in the past as a teacher, through lectures or working groups, but above all through my experience as a preacher: giving the homily, and above all preaching retreats. Most of the time I was addressing young people; they were young people that I was helping to meet the Lord, listen to Him, and also reply to Him.

2. Addressing you now, I would like to do so in such a way as to be able to *answer all your questions, at least indirectly.*

It is for this reason that I cannot do so taking them one after the other. In that case my answers would necessarily be only schematic!

So allow me to choose the question that seems to me the most important, the most central one, and to start with it. In this way, I hope that your other questions will appear gradually.

Your central question concerns Jesus Christ. You want to hear me speak of Jesus Christ, and you ask me who is Jesus Christ for me (it is your 13th question).

Allow me to return the question also and say to you: who is Jesus Christ for you? In this way, and without evading the question, I shall also give you my answer, telling you what He is for me.

3. The whole of the Gospel is a dialogue with man, with the different generations, with nations, with different traditions...but it is always and continually a dialogue with man, with every man, one, unique, absolutely individual.

At the same time, we find many dialogues in the Gospel. Among the latter, I choose as particularly eloquent Christ's dialogue with the young man.

I will read you the text, because perhaps you do not remember it very well. It is in chapter 19 of the Gospel of Matthew.

"And behold, one came up to him, saying, 'Teacher, what good deed must I do, to have eternal life?' And he said to him, 'Why do you ask me about what is good? One there is who is good. If you would enter life, keep the commandments.' He said to him, 'which?' And Jesus said, 'You shall not kill, You shall not commit adultery, You shall not steal, You shall not bear false witness, Honor your father and mother, and, You shall love your neighbor as yourself.' The young man said to him, 'All these I have observed; what do I still lack?' Jesus said to him, 'If you would be perfect, go, sell what you possess and give it to the poor, and you will have treasure in heaven; and come, follow me.' When the young man heard this he went away sorrowful; for he had great possessions."

Why does Christ dialogue with this young man? The answer is found in the Gospel narrative. And you, you ask me why, wherever I go, I want to meet the young (it is even your first question).

And I answer you: because "a young man" indicates a man who, in a special way, in a decisive way, is in the act of "forming himself." That does not mean that man does not form himself for the whole of his life: it is said that "education begins already before birth" and lasts to the last day. From the point of view of formation, however, youth is a particularly important, rich and decisive period. If you reflect on Christ's dialogue with the young man, you will find confirmation of what I have just said.

The young man's questions are essential ones. So are the answers.

4. These questions and these answers are not only essential for the young man concerned, important for his situation at that time; they are also of prime importance and essential for today. That is why, to the question whether the Gospel can answer the problems of modern men (it is your 9th question), I answer: not only "is it capable of doing so," but we must go even further: it alone gives them a total answer, which goes to the bottom of things and completely.

I said at the beginning that Christ is the Word, the Word of an incessant dialogue. He is the *dialogue,* the dialogue with every man, although some people do not take part in it, not everyone knows how to—and there are also people who reject this dialogue explicitly. They move away.... And yet...perhaps this dialogue is in progress with them too. I am convinced that this is so. More than once this dialogue "is revealed" in an unexpected and surprising way.

5. I note also your question why, in the various countries to which I go, and also in Rome, I speak to the various heads of State (question number 2).

Simply because Christ speaks to all men, to every man. Moreover, I think, rest assured, that there is no less to be said to men who have such great social responsibilities as to the young man of the Gospel and to each of you.

To your question, what I speak about when I talk to heads of State, I will reply that I speak to them very often, precisely of the young. In fact, "the day of tomorrow" depends on youth. These words are taken from a song that young Poles of your age often sing "It is on us that the day of tomorrow depends." I, too, have sung it more than once with them. Furthermore, I generally enjoyed very much singing songs with the young, for the music and for the words. I recall this memory because you also asked me questions about my country (it is your 7th question), but to answer this question I should have to speak for a very long time!

And you also ask what France could learn from Poland, and what Poland could learn from France.

It is generally considered that Poland has learned more from France than the latter from Poland. Historically, Poland is several centuries younger. I think, however, that France could also learn various things. Poland has not had an easy history, especially in the course of the last few centuries. The Poles have "paid," and not just a little, in order to be Poles, and also to be Christians.... This answer is an "autobiographical" one. You will excuse me for this, but it was you who caused it. Allow me, however, to widen this autobiographical answer with the help of some other questions that you asked, for example, when you ask if the Church, which is "Western," can really be the "African" or "Asian" Church (20th question).

Who is Jesus Christ for you?... The whole of the Gospel is a dialogue with man, with the different generations, with nations, with different traditions...but it is always and continually a dialogue with man, with every man, one, unique, absolutely individual.

6. Of course, this question is much broader and goes further than the one about which I have just spoken with regard to the Church in France or in Poland. Both of them, in fact, are "Western," belonging to the field of the same European and Latin culture, but my answer will be the same. By her nature, the Church is one and universal. She becomes the Church of every nation, or of continents or races, in proportion as these societies accept the Gospel and make it, so to speak, their property. A short time ago, I went to Africa. Everything indicates that the young Churches of this continent are well aware of being African. And they are consciously aspiring to act as the link between Christianity and the traditions of their cultures. In Asia, and above all in the Far East, it is often thought that Christianity is the "Western" religion, and yet, I do not doubt that the Churches that have taken root there are "Asian" Churches.

7. Let us now return to our main subject, Christ's dialogue with the young man.

Actually, I would be inclined to say that we have remained all the time in its context.

The young man asks, then: "Teacher, what good deed must I do to have eternal life?" (Mt. 19:16)

Now you raise the question: Is it possible to be happy in the modern world?... (it is your 12th question)

As a matter of fact, you ask the same question as this young man!

Christ answers—to him and also to you, to each of you—it is possible. That is, in fact, what He answers, even if His words are the following: "If you would enter life, keep the commandments" (Mt. 19:17). And He will reply further later: "If you would be perfect, go, sell what you possess and give to the poor...and follow me" (cf. Mt. 19:21).

These words mean that man cannot be happy except to the extent to which he is capable of accepting the requirements that his own humanity, his dignity as a man, set him. The requirements that God sets him.

8. In this way, therefore, Christ does not only answer the question whether it is possible to be happy—but He says more: how we can be happy, on what condition. This answer is absolutely original, and it cannot be outdated, it can never be superseded. You must think about it carefully and adapt it to yourselves. Christ's answer consists of two parts. In the first one, it is a question of observing the commandments. Here, I will make a digression on account of one of your questions on the principles that the Church teaches in the field of sexual morality (the 17th question). You express your concern, seeing that they are difficult, and that young people might, precisely for this reason, turn away from the Church. I will answer you as follows. If you think deeply about this question, and if you go to the heart of the problem, I assure you that you will realize one thing: in this field, the Church sets only the requirements that are closely linked with true, that is responsible, married and conjugal love. She demands what the dignity of the person and fundamental social order requires. I do not deny that they are her demands. But the essential point of the problem lies precisely there: namely, that man fulfills himself only to the extent to which he is able to impose demands on himself. Otherwise, he goes away "sorrowful," as we have just read in the

Gospel. Moral permissiveness does not make men happy. The consumer society does not make men happy. They have never done so.

9. In Christ's dialogue with the young man, there are, as I said, two stages. In the first one, it is a question of the Ten Commandments, that is, the fundamental requirements of all human morality. In the second stage, Christ says: "If you would be perfect... come, follow me" (Mt. 9:21).

This "come, follow me" is a central and culminating point of this whole episode. These words indicate that it is not possible to learn Christianity like a lesson composed of numerous different chapters, but that it must always be linked with a Person, a living Person: Jesus Christ. Jesus Christ is the guide; He is the model. We can imitate Him in different ways and to different extents. We can make Him, in different ways and to different extents, the "Rule" of our own lives.

Each of us is a kind of particular "material" from which—following Christ—we can draw this concrete, unique and absolutely individual form of life that can be called the Christian vocation. On this point, a great many things were said at the last Council, as regards the vocation of the laity.

10. That does not change anything about the fact that this "follow me" of Christ's, in the precise case, is and remains the priestly vocation or the vocation to consecrated life according to the evangelical counsels. I say so because you asked the question (the 10th one) about my own priestly vocation. I will try to reply to you briefly, following the pattern of your question. So I will say first of all: I have been Pope for two years; I have been a bishop for over twenty years, and yet the

most important thing for me still remains the fact of being a priest. The fact of being able to celebrate the Eucharist every day. Of being able to renew Christ's own sacrifice, by giving back, in Him, all things to the Father: the world, humanity, and myself. The correct dimension of the Eucharist consists, in fact, in this. That is why I have always living in my memory this interior development as a result of which "I heard" Christ's call to the priesthood, this special "come and follow me."

Confiding this to you, I invite you to listen carefully, each one of you, to these evangelical words. It is in this way that your humanity will be formed completely, and that the Christian vocation of each of you will be defined. And perhaps you will also hear, in your turn, the call to the priesthood or to religious life. Until quite recently, France was rich in these vocations. She has given, among others, so many missionaries and so many missionary sisters to the Church! Certainly, Christ continues to speak on the banks of the Seine, and He always makes the same call. Listen attentively. It will always be necessary so that there may be in the Church those "chosen from among men," those whom Christ appoints, in a special way, on "behalf of men" (Heb. 5:1) and whom He sends to men.

11. You also asked the question about prayer (the 4th one). There are several definitions of prayer. But it is most often called a talk, a conversation, a colloquy with God. Conversing with someone, not only do we speak, but we also listen. Prayer, therefore, is also listening. It consists of listening to hear the interior voice of grace. Listening to hear the call. And then, as you ask me how the Pope prays, I answer

you: like every Christian: he speaks and he listens. Sometimes, he prays without words, and then he listens all the more. The most important thing is precisely what he "hears." And he also tries to unite prayer with his obligations, his activities, his work, and to unite his work with prayer. In this way, day after day, he tries to carry out his "service," his "ministry," which comes to him from the will of Christ and from the living tradition of the Church.

12. You ask me also how I see this service now that I have already been, for two years, Peter's Successor (6th question). I see it above all as a maturation in the priesthood and as permanence in prayer, with Mary, the Mother of Christ, in the same way as the Apostles were assiduous in prayer, in the Upper Room in Jerusalem, when they received the Holy Spirit. In addition to that, you will find my answer to this question on the basis of the replies to the subsequent questions. And first and foremost the one concerning the implementation of the Second Vatican Council (14th question). You ask if it is possible? And I reply to you: not only is the implementation of the Council possible, but it is necessary. This answer is above all the answer of faith. It was the first answer I gave, on the day after my election, in the presence of the Cardinals gathered in the Sistine Chapel. It is the answer I gave myself and others, first as Bishop and as Cardinal, and it is the answer I give continually. It is the main problem. I think that through the Council there were verified for the Church in our time the words of Christ in which He promised His Church the Spirit of truth, who will lead the minds and hearts of the Apostles and their successors, permitting them to remain in the truth and guide the Church in the truth,

rereading "the signs of the times" in the light of this truth. That is precisely what the Council did, in accordance with the needs of our time, of our age. I believe that, thanks to the Council, the Holy Spirit "is speaking" to the Church. I say that taking up again St. John's expression. Our duty is to understand firmly and honestly what "the Spirit says," and to carry it out, avoiding deviations from the road that the Council marked out from so many points of view.

13. The service of the bishop, and in particular that of the Pope, is bound up with a special responsibility as regards what the Spirit says: as regards the whole Faith of the Church and Christian morality. In fact, it is this Faith and this morality that they, the bishops with the Pope, must teach in the Church, watching by the light of Tradition, always alive, over their conformity with the revealed Word of God. That is why they sometimes have to note also that certain opinions or certain publications show that they lack this conformity. They do not constitute an *authentic* doctrine of Christian faith and morality. I speak about this because you asked about it (5th question). If we had more time, a more developed exposition could be devoted to this problem—all the more so in that there is no lack of false information and erroneous explanations in this field, but today we must be content with these few words.

14. The work for the unity of Christians is, in my opinion, one of the greatest and finest tasks of the Church for our age.

You would like to know if I am expecting unity and how I view it? I will answer you the same thing as in connection with the implementation of the Council. There, too, I see a special call of the Holy Spirit.

As regards its implementation, the different stages of this implementation, we find all the fundamental elements in the teaching of the Council. They must be put into practice, and their concrete applications must be sought; and above all it is necessary to pray always, with fervor, constancy and humility. The union of Christians cannot be realized otherwise than through deep maturation in the truth, and a constant conversion of hearts. We must do all that in accordance with our human capacities, taking up again all the "historical processes" that have lasted for centuries. But finally this union, for which we must spare no efforts or work, will be Christ's gift to His Church. Just as it is already one of His gifts that we have already entered upon the way to unity.

15. Continuing with the list of your questions, I reply to you: I have very often spoken of the duties of the Church in the field of justice and peace (15th question), thus continuing the activity of my great Predecessors, John XXIII and Paul VI. Tomorrow in particular, I intend to speak at the headquarters of UNESCO, in Paris. I am referring to all that because you ask: what can we, the young, do for this cause? Can we do something to prevent a new war, a catastrophe that would be incomparable, more terrible than the preceding one? I think that, in the very formulation of your questions, you will find the awaited answer. Read these questions. Meditate on them. Make them a community program, a program of life. You young people have already the possibility of promoting peace and justice, where you are, in your world. That already comprises precise attitudes of kindness in judgment, truth about yourselves and others, their differences, their important rights. In

this way an atmosphere of brotherhood is prepared for the future when you will have greater responsibilities in society. If we wish to make a new and brotherly world, we must prepare new men.

16. And now the question on the Third World (the 8th one). It is a great question concerning history, culture and civilization. But it is above all a moral problem. You rightly ask what must be the relations between your country and the countries of the Third World: of Africa and Asia. There are, in fact, great obligations of a moral nature there. Our "Western" world is at the same time "northern" (European or Atlantic). Its riches and its progress owe a great deal to the resources and men of these continents. In the new situation in which we find ourselves after the Council, it cannot seek there only sources of further riches and of its own progress. It must consciously, and by organizing itself to do so, serve their development. This is perhaps the most important problem as regards justice and peace in the world of today and tomorrow. The solution of this problem depends on the present generation, and it will depend on your generation and on those that will follow. Here, too, it is a question of continuing the witness borne to Christ and the Church by several previous generations of religious and lay missionaries.

17. The question: how to be a witness to Christ today? (18th one) This is the fundamental question, the continuation of the meditation we have placed at the center of our dialogue, the conversation with a young man. Christ says: "Follow me." This is what He said to Simon, the son of Jonas, to whom He gave the name of Peter; to his brother Andrew; to the sons of Zebedee; to Nathanael. He said, "Follow me,"

repeating then, after the resurrection, "you shall be my witnesses" (Acts 1:8). To be a witness to Christ, to bear witness to Him, it is necessary, first, to follow Him. It is necessary to learn to know Him, to place oneself, so to speak, in His school, to penetrate all His mystery. It is a fundamental and central task. If we do not do so, if we are not ready to do so constantly and honestly, our witness runs the risk of becoming superficial and exterior. It runs the risk of no longer being witness. If, on the contrary, we remain attentive to that, Christ Himself will teach us, through His Spirit, what we have to do, how to behave, in what and how to commit ourselves, how to carry on the dialogue with the modern world, this dialogue that Paul VI called the dialogue of salvation.

18. If you ask me consequently: "What must we do in the Church, we above all, the young?" I will reply: learn to know Christ. Constantly. To learn Christ. The unfathomable treasures of wisdom and science are really found in Him. In Him, man, on whom there weigh his limits, his vices, his weakness and his sin, really becomes "the new man": he becomes the man "for others"; he also becomes the glory of God, because the glory of God, as St. Irenaeus of Lyons, bishop and martyr, said in the second century, is "living man." The experience of two millennia teaches us that in this fundamental work, the mission of the whole People of God, there is no essential difference between man and woman. Each in his way, according to the specific characteristics of femininity and masculinity, becomes this "new man," that is, this man "for others," and as a living man he becomes the glory of God. If that is true, just as it is true that the Church, in the hierarchical sense,

is directed by the successors of the Apostles and therefore by men, it is certainly all the more true that, in the charismatic sense, women "lead" her as much, and perhaps even more: I invite you to think often of Mary, the Mother of Christ.

19. Before concluding this testimony based on your questions, I would like to thank again very specially the many representatives of French youth who, before my arrival in Paris, sent me thousands of letters. I thank you for having manifested this bond, this communion, this co-responsibility. I hope that this bond, this communion and this co-responsibility will be continued, and will deepen and develop after our meeting this evening.

I ask you also to strengthen your union with the young people of the whole Church and of the world, in the spirit of this certainty that Christ is our Way, the Truth and the Life (cf. Jn. 14:6).

Let us now unite in this prayer which He Himself taught us, singing "Our Father," and receive, all of you, for yourselves, for boys and girls of your age, for your families and for those who are suffering most, the blessing of the Bishop of Rome, the Successor of St. Peter.

Our Father who art in heaven, hallowed be thy name. Thy kingdom come, thy will be done, on earth as it is in heaven. Give us this day our daily bread, and forgive us our trespasses, as we forgive those who trespass against us; and lead us not into temptation, but deliver us from evil. Amen.

RAISE YOUR EYES TOWARDS JESUS CHRIST!

The address prepared by the Holy Father for the meeting with young Parisians at Parc des Princes, *which was replaced by the one that the Pope actually delivered in reply to the questions submitted to him, was left to the young in the form of a message. The text is as follows.*

Thank you, thank you, dear young people of France, for having come this evening for this vigil with the Pope! Thank you for your trust! I thank, too, all those who have written to me! The meeting with the young is always a very special moment of my pastoral visits. Thank you for what you have prepared this evening for the eyes and for the heart! You now give me your testimony, you profess your faith. And I will then speak of your lives as young people, bearing in mind your questions, and with you I will profess the whole faith of the Church.

Dear young people of France,

1. My hearty thanks for having come in such large numbers, so joyful, so confident, so united with one another! My thanks to the young people of Paris and of the Paris region! My thanks to the young people who have come enthusiastically from all over France!

I would have liked so much to shake hands with each of you, look into your eyes, and say a personal and friendly word. This practical impossibility is not an obstacle to the deep communion of spirits and hearts. Your exchanges of testimonies are the proof.

Your assembly is a delight to my eyes and over-whelms my heart. Your assembly of young people has wished to be worthy of the crowds of young people I have already met in the course of my apostolic jour-neys, in Mexico first of all, then in Poland, in Ireland, in the United States, and recently in Africa. I can con-fide to you: God has bestowed on me—as on so many bishops and priests—the grace of loving the young passionately. Though they are certainly different from one country to another, they are so similar in their enthusiasms and their disappointments, their aspirations and their generosity!

Those of you who have had the possibility of es-tablishing contacts and making friends with young people of another province, another country, another continent than their own, will understand better, perhaps, and certainly share my faith in youth, be-cause they are everywhere, today as yesterday, the bearers of great hopes for the world and for the Church. Young people of France, convinced Christians or sympathizers with Christianity, I would like us, on this unforgettable evening, to make a climb, all roped together, in the direction of the difficult, and at the same time bracing, peaks of the vocation of man, of Christian man. I wish, in fact, to share with you, as a friend with his friends, my own convictions as a man and as a servant of the Faith and unity of the People of God.

AN EXISTENCE REALLY HUMAN

2. Your problems and your sufferings as young people are known to me, at least in general: a certain instability inherent in your age and increased by the acceleration of the changes of history, a certain mistrust with regard to certainties, aggravated by the knowledge learned at school and the frequent atmosphere of systematic criticism, concern about the future and the difficulties of professional integration, the stimulation and superabundance of desires in a society which makes pleasure the purpose of life, the painful feeling of powerlessness to master the ambiguous or fatal consequences of progress, the temptations of revolt, escape or resignation. You know all that, to the extent of being saturated with it. I prefer, with you, to reach the heights. I am convinced that you want to get out of this debilitating atmosphere and deepen or rediscover the meaning of an existence that is really human because it is open to God, in a word, your vocation as a man in Christ.

3. The human being is a corporeal being. This very simple statement is pregnant with consequences. However material it may be, the body is not an object among other objects. It is, in the first place, someone, in the sense that it is a manifestation of the person, a way of being present to others, of communication, of extremely varied expression. The body is a word, a language. What a marvel, and what a risk at the same time! Young men and women, have very great respect for your body and for the bodies of others! Let your body be in the service of your inner self! Let your gestures, your looks, always be the reflection of your soul! Worship of the body? No, never! Contempt for the body? Again no! Control of the body? Yes! Trans-

figuration of the body! Even more! It often happens to you to admire the marvelous transparency of the soul in many men and women in the daily accomplishment of their human tasks. Think of the students and sportsmen who put all their physical energies in the service of their respective ideals. Think of the father and the mother whose faces, bending over their child, reveal so deeply the joys of fatherhood and motherhood. Think of the musician or the actor identified with the authors whom they bring to life again. See the Trappist or the Carthusian, the Carmelite or the Poor Clare, radically abandoned to contemplation and letting God shine through them.

MASTERY OF SELF

I really hope that you will take up the challenge of this time and be, one and all, champions of Christian mastery of the body. Sports, rightly understood, which are springing up again today beyond the circle of professionals, are a very great help. This mastery is decisive for the integration of sexuality in your lives as young people and adults. It is difficult to speak of sexuality at the present time, marked by a lack of inhibitions which is not without an explanation but which is, alas, stimulated by a real exploitation of the sexual instinct. Young people of France, the union of bodies has always been the most forceful language in which two beings can communicate with each other. That is why this language, which touches the sacred mystery of man and woman, demands that the gestures of love should never be performed without the conditions of a complete and definitive assumption of responsibility for the partner, and that the commitment should be undertaken publicly in marriage. Young people of France, preserve or find again a healthy view of corporal values! Contemplate more Christ, the Redeemer of man! He is the Word made flesh whom so many artists have painted with realism in order to signify to us clearly that He assumed everything of human nature, including sexuality, sublimating it in chastity.

A MIND TO THINK

4. The mind is the original element that fundamentally distinguishes man from the animal world and that gives him the power to master the universe. I cannot resist quoting to you your incomparable French writer, Pascal: "Man is only a reed, the weakest one in nature; but he is a thinking reed. It is not necessary for the whole universe to take up arms to crush him...; but even if the universe were to crush him, man would still be nobler than what kills him, because he knows that he is dying; and the universe knows nothing of the advantage it has over him. Our whole dignity, therefore, consists in thought...; so let us work at thinking well" (*Pensées,* no. 347).

Speaking of the mind in this way, I mean the mind capable of understanding, willing, loving. It is precisely through these that man is a man. Safeguard the sacred sphere of the mind at all costs in you and around you! You know that in the modern world there still exist, alas, totalitarian systems which paralyze the mind, and seriously impair the integrity, the identity of man, by reducing him to the state of an object, a machine, by depriving him of his interior resilience, of his impulses of freedom and love. You know also that there are economic systems which, while priding themselves on their formidable industrial expansion, accentuate, at the same time, the degradation, the decomposition of man. Even the mass media, which should contribute to the complete development of men and to their mutual enrichment in growing brotherhood, are sometimes guilty of hammering at the intelligence and the imagination and even bewitching them, in a way that is harmful to the health of the mind, of judgment and of the heart, and distorts man's capacity of discerning what is healthy from what is unhealthy.

Yes, what is the use of social and political reforms, even very generous ones, if the mind, which is also conscience, loses its lucidity and its vigor? In practice, in the world such as it is and which you must not flee, learn more and more to reflect, to think! The studies that you are carrying out must be a very special moment of apprenticeship to the life of the mind. Unmask slogans, false values, mirages, dead ends! I wish you the spirit of meditation, of interiority. Each one of you, at his or her level, must promote the primacy of the spirit and even contribute to bringing back into honor what has value for eternity even more than for the future. Living in this way, believers or non-believers, you are all close to God. God is Spirit!

A HEART TO LOVE

5. You are also worth what your heart is worth. The whole history of mankind is the history of the need of loving and being loved. This end of the century —especially in regions of accelerated social change— makes the development of healthy emotions more dif-

ficult. That is probably why many young and not so young people seek the atmosphere of little groups, in order to escape from anonymity and sometimes from distress, in order to find again their deep vocation for interpersonal relations. If we are to believe a certain type of advertising, our age is even enamored of what could be called a doping of the heart.

It is important in this sphere, as in the preceding ones, to see things clearly. Whatever use humans make of it, the heart—the symbol of friendship and love—has also its norms, its ethics. To make room for the heart in the harmonious construction of your personality has nothing to do with mawkishness or even sentimentality. The heart is the opening of the whole being to the existence of others, the capacity of divining them, of understanding them. Such a sensitiveness, true and deep, makes one vulnerable. That is why some people are tempted to get rid of it by hardening their hearts.

To love is, therefore, essentially to give oneself to others. Far from being an instinctive inclination, love is a conscious decision of the will to go towards others. To be able to love truly, it is necessary to detach oneself from many things and above all from oneself, to give gratuitously, to love to the end. This dispossession of oneself—a long and demanding task—is exhausting and exalting. It is the source of balance. It is the secret of happiness.

Young people of France, raise your eyes more often towards Jesus Christ! He is the Man who loved most, and most consciously, most voluntarily and most gratuitously! Meditate on Christ's testament: "There is no greater proof of love than to give one's life for those one loves." Contemplate the Man-God,

To love is essentially to give oneself to others. Far from being an instinctive inclination, love is a conscious decision of the will to go towards others. To be able to love truly, it is necessary to detach oneself from many things and above all from oneself, to give gratuitously, to love to the end. This dispossession of oneself—a long and demanding task—is exhausting and exalting. It is the source of balance. It is the secret of happiness.

the Man with the pierced heart! Do not be afraid! Jesus did not come to condemn love but to free love from its ambiguities and its counterfeits. It was He who changed the heart of Zacchaeus, of the Samaritan woman, and who still operates similar conversions today, all over the world. It seems to me that tonight, Christ is whispering to each one of you: "Give me your heart!... I will purify it, I will strengthen it, I will turn it towards all those who need it: towards your own family, your school or university community, your social environment, towards the unloved, towards foreigners living on the soil of France, towards the inhabitants of the Third World who do not have enough to live on and to develop, towards the most humble of men. Love demands sharing!"

Young people of France, it is more than ever the time to work hand-in-hand at the civilization of love, according to the expression dear to my great Predecessor, Paul VI. What a gigantic workyard! What a stirring task!

On the plane of the heart, of love, I have something else to confide to you. I believe with my whole strength that many of you are capable of risking the complete gift, to Christ and to their brothers, of all their powers of loving. You understand perfectly that I mean the vocation to the priesthood and to the religious life. Your towns and villages in France are waiting for ministers with hearts burning to proclaim the Gospel, celebrate the Eucharist, reconcile sinners with God and with their brothers. They are also waiting for women radically consecrated to the service of Christian communities and their human and spiritual needs. Your answer to this call lies along the direct line of Christ's last question to Peter: "Do you love me?"

MYSTERY OF CHRIST'S LOVE FOR US

6. I have spoken of the values of the heart, the mind and the heart. But at the same time I have given glimpses of an essential dimension without which man becomes again a prisoner of himself or of others: it is openness to God. Yes, without God, man loses the key to himself, he loses the key to his history. For, since creation, he has borne within him the likeness of God. This remains in him in the state of an implicit wish and unconscious need, in spite of sin. And man is destined to live with God. There, too, Christ will reveal Himself as our Way. But this mystery requires, perhaps, greater attention.

Jesus Christ, the Son of God made man, lived everything that constitutes the value of our human nature, body, mind and heart, in a fully free relationship with others, marked by the seal of truth and filled with love. His whole life, as much as His words, manifested this freedom, this truth, this love, and especially the voluntary gift of His life for men. In this way He was able to proclaim the charter of a blessed world, yes blessed, on the way of poverty, sweetness, justice, hope, mercy, purity, peace, faithfulness even in persecution, and two thousand years afterwards, this charter is inscribed in the heart of our gathering. But Christ did not only give an example and teach. He actually freed men and women from what held their bodies, their minds and their hearts captive. And since His death and resurrection for us, He continues to do so, for men and women from all walks of life and from all countries, from the moment when they give Him their faith. He is the Savior of man. He is the Redeemer of man. *"Ecce homo,"* Pilate said, without being clearly conscious of the significance of his words: "There is the man."

How do we dare to say that, dear friends? Christ's earthly life was a short one, His public life even shorter. But His life is unique, His personality is unique in the world. He is not only a Brother for us, a Friend, a Man of God. We recognize in Him the only Son of God, who is one with God the Father and whom the Father gave to the world. With the apostle Peter, whose humble Successor I am, I profess: "You are the Christ, the Son of the living God." It is precisely because Christ shares at once the divine nature and our human nature that the offering of His life, in His death and His resurrection, reaches us, the men of today, saves us, purifies us, frees us, elevates us: "The Son of God in a certain way united Himself with each man." And I like to repeat here the wish of my first encyclical. "That each person may be able to find Christ, in order that Christ may walk with each person the path of life, with the power of truth about man and the world that is contained in the mystery of the Incarnation and the Redemption and with the power of the love that is radiated by that truth" (*Redemptor hominis,* no. 13).

If Christ liberates and raises our humanity, it is because He introduces it into the covenant with God, with the Father, with the Son, and with the Holy Spirit. This morning we celebrated the feast of the Holy Trinity. That is the real opening to God to which every human heart aspires even without knowing it and which Christ offers the believer. It is a question of a personal God and not just the God of philosophers and scholars; it is the God revealed in the Bible, the God of Abraham, the God of Jesus Christ, He who is at the heart of our history. He is the God who can seize all the resources of your body, your mind and your heart, to make them bear fruit, in a word, who can seize your whole being to renew it in Christ, now and beyond death.

That is my faith, that has been the faith of the Church since the origins, the only one that is founded on the witness of the Apostles, the only one that resists fluctuations, the only one that saves man. I am sure that many of you have already experienced it. May they find in my coming an encouragement to deepen it by all the means that the Church puts at their disposal.

Others are undoubtedly more hesitant to adhere fully to this faith. Some consider themselves to be unbelievers and perhaps incapable of believing, or indifferent to faith. Others still reject a God whose face has been badly presented to them. Others, finally, shaken by the fall-out of philosophies of suspicion which present religion as an illusion or alienation, are perhaps tempted to construct a humanism without God. I hope, however, that all those will at least, out of honesty, leave their window open to God. Otherwise, they run the risk of missing the way to man which Christ is, of shutting themselves up in attitudes of revolt and violence, of contenting themselves with sighs of helplessness or resignation. A world without God is constructed, sooner or later, against man. Certainly, many social or cultural influences, many personal events, may have obstructed your way to faith, or turned you away from it. But actually, if you wish, in the midst of these difficulties which I understand, you have still, finally, a good chance, in your country of religious freedom, to clear this way and have access, with the grace of God, to faith! You have the means to do so! Are you really taking them? In the name of all the love that I bear you, I do not hesitate to call upon you: "Throw open your doors to Christ!" What do you fear? Trust Him. Take the risk of following Him. That requires, of course, that you should come out of yourselves, your reasonings, your "wisdom," your indifference, your self-complacency, the non-Christian habits that you may have acquired. Yes, that calls for sacrifice, a conversion, which you must first dare to desire, ask in prayer and begin to practice. Let Christ be for you the Way, the Truth, and the Life. Let Him be your salvation and your happiness. Let him seize your whole life in order that it may reach all its dimensions with Him, that all your relationships, activities, feelings and thoughts may be integrated in Him, one could say "Christified." I hope that with Christ you will recognize God as the source and end of your existence.

These are the men and women that the world needs, that France needs. You will personally have the happiness promised in the Beatitudes and you will be, in all humility and respect for others, and in their midst, the leaven of which the Gospel speaks. You will build a new world; you will prepare a Christian future. It is a way of the cross, yes, it is also a way of joy, for it is a way of hope.

With all my trust and all my affection I call upon the young people of France to raise their heads and walk together along this way, their hands in the Lord's hand. "Arise, young woman! Arise, young man!"

Let Christ be for you the Way, the Truth, and the Life. Let Him be your salvation and your happiness. Let Him seize your whole life in order that it may reach all its dimensions with Him, that all your relationships, activities, feelings and thoughts may be integrated in Him, one could say "Christified."

With all my trust and all my affection I call upon the young people of France to raise their heads and walk together along this way, their hands in the Lord's hand. "Arise, young woman! Arise, young man!"

HERE IS THAT HEART WHICH LOVED MEN SO MUCH

After the meeting with the young people of Paris, the Holy Father went late at night on Sunday, June 1, to the Basilica of the Sacred Heart in Montmartre, for a pause of prayer and reflection.

This is the text of the Pope's meditation.

1. " Stay with us, Lord, for the day is now far spent" (cf. Lk. 24:29). The disciples of Emmaus had their hearts already burning within them after having heard the marvels in the Scriptures explained to them on the way. With the breaking of bread, the Lord concludes the revelation to them of Himself, risen again, in the fullness of His love.

We are at Montmartre, in the Basilica of the Sacred Heart, consecrated to the contemplation of Christ's love present in the Blessed Sacrament.

We are in the evening of the first of June, the first day of the month particularly dedicated to meditation, to contemplation of Christ's love manifested by His Sacred Heart.

Here, day and night, Christians gather in succession to seek "the unsearchable riches of Christ" (cf. Eph. 3:8).

2. We come here to meet the heart pierced for us, from which water and blood gush. It is the redeeming love, which is at the origin of salvation, of our salvation, which is at the origin of the Church.

We come here to contemplate the love of the Lord Jesus: His compassionate kindness to everyone during His earthly life; His predilection for children, the sick, the afflicted. Let us contemplate His heart burning with love for His Father, in the fullness of the Holy Spirit. Let us contemplate His infinite love, that of the eternal Son, who leads us to the very mystery of God.

3. Now still, today, the living Christ loves us and presents His heart to us as the source of our redemption: *Semper vivens ad interpellandum pro nobis* (Heb. 7:25). At every moment, we are enveloped, the whole world is enveloped, in the love of this heart "which loved men so much and which is so little loved by them."

"I live," St. Paul says, "by faith in the Son of God, who loved me and gave himself for me" (Gal. 2:20). Meditation on the Lord's love is bound to pass through meditation on His passion: "He gave himself for me." This implies that each one should become aware not only of the sin of the world in general, but of this sin through which each one is really involved, negatively, in the Lord's sufferings.

This meditation on love manifested in the passion must also lead us to live in conformity with the requirements of Baptism, to this purification of our being by the water that gushed from Christ's heart; to live in accordance with the appeal He makes to us every day through His grace. May He grant us now the privilege "of keeping watch and praying" in order

not to succumb to temptation. May He grant us the
privilege of entering His mystery spiritually; of hav
ing in us, as St. Paul said further, the sentiments tha
were in Christ Jesus... "who became obedient unte
death" (Phil. 2:5-8).

Thereby, we are called to respond fully to His
love, and to dedicate our activities, our apostolate
our whole life, to Him.

4. We are called not only to meditate on, and con
template, this mystery of Christ's love; we are called
to take part in it. It is the mystery of the Holy
Eucharist, the center of our faith, the center of our
worship of Christ's merciful love manifested in His
Sacred Heart, a mystery which is adored here nigh
and day, in this basilica, which thereby becomes one
of these centers from which the Lord's love and grace
radiate in a mysterious but real way on your city, on
your country and on the redeemed world.

In the Holy Eucharist, we celebrate the ever new
and active presence of the one sacrifice of the cross in
which Redemption is an event eternally present, in
dissolubly linked with the very intercession of the
Savior.

In the Holy Eucharist, we commune with Christ
Himself, the one Priest and the one Host, who bears
us along in the movement of His offering and His wor
ship, He who is the source of all grace.

In the Holy Eucharist—this is also the meaning of
perpetual worship—we enter this movement of love
from which all interior progress and all apostolic ef
ficacy springs: "And I, when I am lifted up from the
earth, will draw all men to myself" (Jn. 12:32).

Dear brothers and sisters, my joy is great to be
able to end this day in this exalted place of Eucharistic

prayer, in your midst, gathered by love for the divine heart. Pray to it. Live by this message which, from the Gospel of St. John at Paray-le-Monial, calls us to enter its mystery. May we all "draw water from the wells of salvation with joy" (cf. Is. 12:3), those that spring from the love of the Lord, who died and rose again for us.

It is to Him that, this evening too, I commend your country and all your apostolic intentions. I willingly give you my blessing.

CATHOLICS AT THE SERVICE OF INTERNATIONAL RELATIONS

At 8:30 a.m. on June 2, the Holy Father arrived at the Poor Clares' Chapel where he met the representatives of the International Catholic Organizations (I.C.O.) accredited to UNESCO, and addressed them as follows:

My dear brothers and sisters in Christ,

1. In the framework of my visit to UNESCO, I wished to meet also the representatives of the International Catholic Organizations (I.C.O.) and of the International Catholic Center for UNESCO. I know that you are following closely, according to the status that you are granted as non-governmental organizations, the activities of this organization of the United Nations. I thank you for your presence and your interest.

As I did in New York on the occasion of my visit to the United Nations Organization, I wish to stress through my presence at UNESCO the interest that the Holy See takes in the life of international organizations, in meetings at which the major problems of the contemporary world are discussed, and in the multiple efforts of international cooperation which aim at promoting on the world scale a life in common marked by justice and respect for inalienable human rights. For, as my Predecessor John XXIII, who was the first of the permanent observers of the Holy See to UNESCO, said in his encyclical *Pacem in terris*, socialization at the world level is a fact. This reality requires more than ever that a new order of international relations be established on the basis of an ethics of justice, respect for the human person, recognition of the sovereignty of every nation, and solidarity.

2. In this context, it is necessary to promote exchanges among the peoples in order to enable each of them to give itself an identity of its own, founded on a dynamic conception of culture, which plunges its roots in the past, is nourished by the various historical contributions and becomes the creator of new expressions, while remaining faithful to its own values and at the same time open to those of others as well as to a future of progress.

The Church cannot remain alien to this enterprise, she who, by reason of her particular condition, is not bound up with perspectives of political power or economic interest, but is inspired solely by the mission that Christ has entrusted to her.

In fact, by virtue of her mandate from Christ to proclaim the Gospel to all peoples, the Church is present in all nations and cultures as the universal sacrament of salvation and unity for mankind. Through her, humanity is reconciled with the Father; through her, brotherhood in Christ is open to all men; through her, finally, the Gospel impregnates moral and religious energies and makes an original contribution to the establishment of a culture, a civilization based on the primacy of the spirit, justice and love.

3. In this perspective, I express my esteem and encouragement to all Catholics who assume their due

responsibility in international life, either, as many among you here, in the service of UNESCO, or, in quite a special way, in the International Catholic Organizations, which have clearly realized what an important role they have to play in this sphere.

Indeed, whether it is a question of the study of great international problems or of making public opinion aware of them and forming it, an irreplaceable contribution is made by the International Catholic Organizations through their status as non-governmental organizations, as well as by the centers of the conference of I.C.O.

I do not underestimate at all the necessity of technical capacities to tackle the delicate and complex problems that arise in the international field. But your specific contribution must consist in the effort to put always at the heart of these problems, where the destiny of men and peoples is at stake, an ethical and religious dimension which is a fundamental element of human reality. No solution is possible through negotiations on the political, economic or technical level—however necessary they may be—if it is not inspired by these fundamental dimensions. Let respect and tolerance, the desire for loyal collaboration and dialogue never be an alibi to conceal or minimize the original contribution that must be yours, on the basis of the truth of Christ, the source of truth about man and his dignity.

4. This contribution will be all the more effective if it can be based on the experiences and reflections that reach you from the grassroots of your organizations and movements, in different places, countries and continents. That is a positive aspect of the I.C.O. By their structure and the origin of their members,

they will be able at the same time to go beyond the horizons of a limited nationalism or regionalism, while avoiding also an imperfect view and practice of internationalism, seen as the privilege of the elite or the powerful or the exclusive field of specialists. Through the extension of their presence in all geographical and cultural environments, through the density of their local and national circuits of coordination and information, through their deep communion with the Church at all levels at which international cooperation is effected, International Catholic Organizations already give and must give more and more a testimony and an important contribution to the building of the city of men and of the kingdom of God.

Dear friends, dear brothers and sisters, may the Lord bless you, you and your families, may He bless your work at UNESCO, and all the *Christi fideles* of the Catholic organizations which you represent.

MAN'S ENTIRE HUMANITY IS EXPRESSED IN CULTURE

On Monday, June 2, John Paul II met the representatives of UNESCO and delivered the following address.

Mr. President of the General Conference,
Mr. President of the Executive Council,
Mr. Director General,
Ladies and gentlemen,

1. I wish in the first place to express my very cordial thanks for the invitation that Mr. Amadou Mahtar-M'Bow, Director General of the United Nations Educational, Scientific and Cultural Organization, extended to me several times, even at the first of the visits he has done me the honor of paying me. There are many reasons for which I am happy to be able to accept today this invitation, which I highly appreciated immediately.

For the kind words of welcome they have just addressed to me, I thank Mr. Napoléon Leblanc, President of the General Conference; Mr. Chams Eldine El-Wakil, President of the Executive Council; and Mr. Amadou Mahtar-M'Bow, Director General of the organization. I also wish to greet all those who are gathered here for the 109th session of UNESCO's Executive Council. I cannot conceal my joy at seeing gathered on this occasion so many delegates from nations all over the world, so many eminent personalities, so many authorities, so many illustrious representatives of the world of culture and science.

Through my intervention, I will try to bring my modest stone to the edifice you are constructing with assiduity and perseverance, ladies and gentlemen, through your reflections and your resolutions in all the fields that are in UNESCO's sphere of competence.

2. Allow me to begin by referring to the origins of your organization. The events that marked the foundation of UNESCO inspire me with joy and gratitude to divine Providence: the signature of its constitution on November 16, 1945; the coming into force of this constitution and the establishment of the organization on November 4, 1946; the agreement between UNESCO and the United Nations Organization approved by the General Assembly of the U.N. in the same year. Your organization is, in fact, the work of the nations which, after the end of the terrible Second World War, were impelled by what could be called a spontaneous desire for peace, union and reconciliation. These nations looked for the means and the forms of a collaboration capable of establishing this new understanding and of deepening it and ensuring it in a lasting way. So UNESCO came into being, like the United Nations Organization, because the peoples knew that at the basis of the great enterprises intended to serve peace and the progress of humanity over the whole globe, there was the necessity of the union of nations, mutual respect and international cooperation.

3. Prolonging the action, thought and message of my great Predecessor, Pope Paul VI, I had the honor of speaking before the United Nations General Assembly, in the month of last October, at the invitation of Mr. Kurt Waldheim, Secretary General of the U.N. Shortly afterwards, on November 12, 1979, I was invited by Mr. Edouard Saouma, Director General of the United Nations Food and Agricultural Organization in Rome. On these occasions I had the honor of dealing with questions deeply linked with all the problems connected with man's peaceful future on earth. In fact, all these problems are closely linked. We are in the presence, so to speak, of a vast system of communicating vessels: the problems of culture, science and education do not arise, in the life of nations and in international relations, independently of the other problems of human existence, such as those of peace or hunger. The problems of culture are conditioned by the other dimensions of human existence, just as the latter, in their turn, condition them.

4. All the same there is—and I stressed it in my address to the U.N., referring to the Universal Declaration of Human Rights—one fundamental dimension, which is capable of shaking to their very foundations the systems that structure mankind as a whole and of freeing human existence, individual and collective, from the threats that weigh on it. This fundamental dimension is man, man in his integrality, man who lives at the same time in the sphere of material values and in that of spiritual values. Respect for the inalienable rights of the human person is at the basis of everything (cf. Address to the U.N., nos. 7, 13).

Any threat to human rights, whether in the framework of man's spiritual goods or in that of his material goods, does violence to this fundamental dimension. That is why, in my address to FAO, I emphasized that no man, no country and no system in the world can remain indifferent to the "geography of hunger" and the gigantic threats that will ensue if the whole direction of economic policy, and in particular the hierarchy of investments, do not change in an essential and radical way. That is also why, referring to the origins of your organization, I stress the necessity of mobilizing all forces which direct the spiritual dimension of human existence, and which bear witness to the primacy of the spiritual in man—and of what corresponds to the dignity of his intelligence, his will and his heart—in order not to succumb again to the monstrous alienation of collective evil, which is always ready to use material powers in the exterminating struggle of men against men, of nations against nations.

5. At the origin of UNESCO, as also at the basis of the Universal Declaration on Human Rights, there are, therefore, these first noble impulses of human conscience, intelligence and will. I appeal to this origin, to this beginning, to these premises and to these first principles. It is in their name that I come today to Paris, to the headquarters of your organization, with an entreaty: that at the end of a stage of over thirty years of your activities, you will unite even more round these ideals and principles on which the beginning was based. It is in their name also that I shall now take the liberty of proposing to you some really fundamental considerations, for it is only by their light that there shines forth fully the meaning of this institution, which has as its name UNESCO, the United Nations Educational, Scientific and Cultural Organization.

6. *"Genus humanum arte et ratione vivit"* (cf. Saint Thomas, commenting on Aristotle, in *Post. Analyt.*, no. 1). These words of one of the greatest geniuses of Christianity, who was at the same time a fruitful continuer of the thought of antiquity, take us beyond the circle of contemporary meaning of Western culture, whether it is Mediterranean or Atlantic. They have a meaning that applies to humanity as a whole, where the different traditions that constitute its spiritual heritage and the different periods of its culture meet. The essential meaning of culture consists, according to these words of St. Thomas Aquinas, in the fact that it is a characteristic of human life as such. Man lives a really human life thanks to culture. Human life is culture in this sense too that, through it, man is distinguished and differentiated from everything that exists elsewhere in the visible world: man cannot do without culture.

Culture is a specific way of man's "existing" and "being." Man always lives according to a culture which is specifically his, and which, in its turn, creates among men a tie which is also specifically theirs, determining the inter-human and social character of human existence. In the unity of culture as the specific way of human existence, there is rooted at the same time the plurality of cultures in the midst of which man lives. In this plurality, man develops without losing, however, the essential contact with the unity of culture as the fundamental and essential dimension of his existence and his being.

7. Man who, in the visible world, is the only ontic subject of culture, is also its only object and its term. Culture is that through which man, as man, becomes more man, "is" more, has more access to "being."

The fundamental distinction between what man is and what he has, between being and having, has its foundation there, too. Culture is always in an essential and necessary relationship to what man is, whereas its relationship to what he has, to his "having," is not only secondary, but entirely relative. All man's "having" is important for culture, is a factor creative of culture, only to the extent to which man, through his "having," can at the same time "be" more fully as a man, become more fully a man in all the dimensions of his existence, in everything that characterizes his humanity. The experience of the various eras, without excluding the present one, proves that people think of culture and speak about it in the first place in relation to the nature of man, then only in a secondary and indirect way in relation to the world of his products. That in no way detracts from the fact that we judge the phenomenon of culture on the basis of what man produces, or that we draw from that, at the same time, conclusions about man. Such an approach—a typical way of the *a posteriori* process of knowledge—contains in itself the possibility of going back, in the opposite direction, to ontic-causal dependencies. Man, and only man, is the "protagonist," or "architect" of culture; man, and only man, expresses himself in it and finds his own balance in it.

THE COMPLETE MAN
THE SUBJECT OF CULTURE

8. All of us present here meet on the ground of culture, the fundamental reality which unites us and which is at the basis of the establishment and purposes of UNESCO. We thereby meet around man

and, in a certain sense, in him, in man. This man, who expresses himself and objectivizes himself in and through culture, is unique, complete and indivisible. He is at once subject and architect of culture. Consequently, he cannot be envisaged solely as the resultant —to give only one example—of the production relations that prevail at a given period. Is this criterion of production relations not at all, then, a key to the understanding of man's historicity, to the understanding of his culture and of the multiple forms of his development? Certainly, this criterion is a key, and even a precious key, but it is not the fundamental, constitutive one. Human cultures reflect, there is no doubt, the various systems of production relations; however, it is not such and such a system that is at the origin of culture, but man, man who lives in the system, who accepts it or tries to change it. A culture without human subjectivity and without human causality is inconceivable; in the cultural field, man is always the first fact: man is the prime and fundamental fact of culture.

And he is so, always, in his totality: in his spiritual and material subjectivity as a complete whole. If the distinction between spiritual culture and material culture is correct with respect to the character and content of the products in which the culture is manifested, it is necessary to note at the same time that, on the one hand, the works of material culture always show a "spiritualization of matter," a submission of the material element to man's spiritual forces— that is, his intelligence and will—and that, on the other hand, the works of spiritual culture manifest, specifically, a "materialization" of the spirit, an incarnation of what is spiritual. In cultural works, this double

characteristic seems to be equally of prime importance and equally permanent.

Here is, therefore, by way of theoretical conclusion, a sufficient basis to understand culture through
the complete man, through the whole reality of his
subjectivity. Here is also—in the field of action—a sufficient basis to seek always in culture the complete
man, the whole man, in the whole truth of his spiritual and corporeal subjectivity; the basis which is sufficient in order not to superimpose on culture—a truly
human system, a splendid synthesis of spirit and
body—preconceived divisions and oppositions. In
fact, whether it is a question of an absolutization of
matter in the structure of the human subject, or, in-
versely, of an absolutization of the spirit in this same
structure, neither expresses the truth about man or
serves his culture.

9. I would like to stop here at another essential
consideration, a reality of a quite different order. We
can approach it by noting the fact that the Holy See is
represented at UNESCO by its permanent observer,
whose presence is set in the perspective of the very
nature of the Apostolic See. This presence is, even
more widely, in harmony with the nature and mission
of the Catholic Church and, indirectly, with that of
the whole of Christianity. I take the opportunity
which is offered to me today to express a deep personal conviction. The presence of the Apostolic See in
your organization—though motivated also by the specific sovereignty of the Holy See—has its justification
above all in the organic and constitutive link which
exists between religion in general and Christianity in
particular, on the one hand, and culture, on the other
hand. This relationship extends to the multiple

realities which must be defined as concrete expressions of culture in the different periods of history and all over the world. It will certainly not be an exaggeration to state in particular that, through a multitude of facts, the whole of Europe—from the Atlantic to the Urals—bears witness, in the history of each nation as in that of the whole community, to the link between culture and Christianity.

Recalling this, it is not at all my intention to belittle the heritage of other continents, or the specific character and value of this same heritage which is derived from the other sources of religious, humanistic and ethical inspiration. What is more, I wish to pay the deepest and most sincere tribute to all the cultures of the human family as a whole, from the most ancient to the contemporary. It is in thinking of all cultures that I wish to say in a loud voice, here in Paris, at the headquarters of UNESCO, with respect and admiration: "Here is man!" I wish to proclaim my admiration before the creative riches of the human spirit, before its incessant efforts to know and strengthen the identity of man: this man who is always present in all the particular forms of culture.

10. Speaking, on the contrary, of the place of the Church and of the Apostolic See in your organization, I am thinking not only of all the works of culture in which, in the course of the last two millennia, the man who had accepted Christ and the Gospel expressed himself, or of the institutions of different kinds that came into being from the same inspiration in the fields of education, instruction, charity, social work and in so many others. I am thinking above all, ladies and gentlemen, of the fundamental link between the Gospel, that is, the message of Christ and

the Church, and man in his very humanity. This link is in fact a creator of culture in its very foundation. To create culture, it is necessary to consider, to its last consequences and entirety, man as a particular and autonomous value, as the subject bearing the transcendency of the person. Man must be affirmed for himself, and not for any other motive or reason: solely for himself! What is more, man must be loved because he is man; love must be claimed for man by reason of the particular dignity he possesses. The whole of the affirmations concerning man belongs to the very substance of Christ's message and of the mission of the Church, in spite of all that critics may have declared about this matter, and all that the different movements opposed to religion in general and to Christianity in particular may have done.

In the course of history, we have already been more than once, and we still are, witnesses of a process of a very significant phenomenon. Where religious institutions have been suppressed, where ideas and works born of religious inspiration, and in particular of Christian inspiration, have been deprived of their citizenship, men find again these same elements outside institutional ways, through the confrontation operated, in truth and interior effort, between what constitutes their humanity and what is contained in the Christian message.

Ladies and gentlemen, you will kindly forgive my making this statement. Proposing it, I did not want to offend anyone at all. I beg you to understand that, in the name of what I am, I could not abstain from giving this testimony. It also bears within it this truth—which cannot be passed over in silence—regarding culture, if we seek in it everything that is human, the elements in which man expresses himself or through which he wants to be the subject of his existence. And in so speaking, I wanted at the same time to manifest all the more my gratitude for the ties that unite UNESCO with the Apostolic See, these ties of which my presence today is intended as a particular expression.

·11. A certain number of fundamental conclusions can be drawn from all that. In fact, the considerations I have just made show clearly that the primary and essential task of culture in general, and also of all culture, is education. Education consists in fact in enabling man to become more man, to "be" more and not just to "have" more and consequently, through everything he "has," everything he possesses, to "be" man more fully. For this purpose man must be able to "be more" not only "with others," but also "for others." Education is of fundamental importance for the formation of inter-human and social relations. Here, too, I touch upon a set of axioms on the basis of which the traditions of Christianity that have sprung from the Gospel meet the educative experience of so many well-disposed and deeply wise men, so numerous in all centuries of history. In our age, too, there is no lack of them, of these men who reveal themselves as great, simply through their humanity which they are able to share with others, in particular with the young. At the same time, the symptoms of crises of all kinds to which there succumb environments and societies which are among those best-off in other ways—crises which affect above all young generations—vie with each other in bearing witness that the work of man's education is not carried out only with the help of institutions, with the help of organized and material means, however excellent they may be.

Education consists, in fact, in enabling man to become more man, to "be" more and not just to "have" more and consequently, through everything he "has," everything he possesses, to "be" man more fully. For this purpose man must be able to "be more" not only "with others," but also "for others." Education is of fundamental importance for the formation of inter-human and social relations.

They also show that the most important thing is always man, man and his moral authority which comes from the truth of his principles and from the conformity of his actions with these principles.

12. As the world organization most competent in all problems of culture, UNESCO cannot neglect this other question which is absolutely fundamental: what can be done in order that man's education may be carried out above all in the family?

What is the state of public morality which will ensure the family, and above all the parents, the moral authority necessary for this purpose? What type of instruction? What forms of legislation sustain this authority or, on the contrary, weaken it or destroy it? The causes of success and failure in the formation of man by his family always lie both within the fundamental creative environment of culture which the family is, and also at a higher level, that of the competence of the state and the organs, on which these causes depend. These problems cannot but cause reflection and solicitude in the forum where the qualified representatives of the state meet.

There is no doubt that the first and fundamental cultural fact is the spiritually mature man, that is, a fully educated man, a man capable of educating himself and educating others. Nor is there any doubt that the first and fundamental dimension of culture is healthy morality: moral culture.

13. Certainly, there are many particular questions in this field, but experience shows that everything is connected, and that these questions are set in systems that plainly depend upon one another. For example, in the process of education as a whole, and of scholastic education in particular, has there not been a

unilateral shift towards instruction in the narrow sense of the word? If we consider the proportions assumed by this phenomenon, as well as the systematic increase of instruction which refers solely to what man possesses, is not man himself put more and more in the shade? That leads, then, to a real alienation of education: instead of working in favor of what man must "be," it works solely in favor of what man can take advantage of in the field of "having," of "possession." The further stage of this alienation is to accustom man, by depriving him of his own subjectivity, to being the object of multiple manipulations: ideological or political manipulations which are carried out through public opinion; those that are operated through monopoly or control, through economic forces or political powers, and the media of social communication; finally, the manipulation which consists of teaching life as a specific manipulation of oneself.

THE APPARENT IMPERATIVES OF OUR SOCIETY

These dangers in the field of education seem to threaten above all societies with a more developed technical civilization. These societies are confronted with man's specific crisis which consists of a growing lack of confidence with regard to his own humanity, to the meaning of the fact of being a man, and to the affirmation and joy derived from it, which are a source of creation. Modern civilization tries to impose on man a series of apparent imperatives, which its spokesmen justify by recourse to the principle of development and progress. Thus, for example, instead of respect for life, "the imperative" of getting rid of life and destroying it; instead of love which is the responsible communion of persons, "the imperative" of the maximum sexual enjoyment apart from any sense of responsibility; instead of the primacy of truth in actions, the "primacy" of behavior that is fashionable, of the subjective, and of immediate success.

In all that there is indirectly expressed a great systematic renunciation of the healthy ambition of being a man. Let us be under no illusions: the system constructed on the basis of these false imperatives, these fundamental renunciations, may determine the future of man and the future of culture.

14. If, in the name of the future of culture, it must be proclaimed that man has the right to "be" more, and if for the same reason it is necessary to demand a healthy primacy of the family in the overall work of educating man to real humanity, the law of the nation must be set along the same line; it, too, must be placed at the basis of culture and education.

The nation is, in fact, the great community of men who are united by various ties, but above all, precisely by culture. The nation exists *through* culture and *for* culture, and it is therefore the great educator of men in order that they may "be more" in the community. It is this community which possesses a history that goes beyond the history of the individual and the family. It is also in this community, with respect to which every family educates, that the family begins its work of education with what is the most simple thing, language, thus enabling man who is at the very beginning to learn to speak in order to become a member of the community of his family and of his nation.

In all that I am now proclaiming, which I will develop still further, my words express a particular experience, a particular testimony in its kind. I am the son of a nation which has lived the greatest experiences of history, which its neighbors have condemned to death several times, but which has survived and remained itself. It has kept its identity, and it has kept, in spite of partitions and foreign occupations, its national sovereignty, not by relying on the resources of physical power, but solely by relying on its culture. This culture turned out in the circumstances to be more powerful than all other forces.

What I say here concerning the right of the nation to the foundation of its culture and its future is not, therefore, the echo of any "nationalism," but it is always a question of a stable element of human experience and of the humanistic perspective of man's development. There exists a fundamental sovereignty of society which is manifested in the culture of the nation. It is a question of the sovereignty through which, at the same time, man is supremely sovereign. When I express myself in this way, I am also thinking, with deep interior emotion, of the cultures of so many ancient peoples which did not give way when confronted with the civilizations of the invaders: and they still remain for man the source of his "being" as a man in the interior truth of his humanity. I am also thinking with admiration of the cultures of new societies, those that are awakening to life in the community of their own nation—just as my nation awakened to life ten centuries ago—and that are struggling to maintain their own identity and their own values against the influences and pressure of models proposed from outside.

15. Addressing you, ladies and gentlemen, you who have been meeting in this place for over thirty years now in the name of the primacy of the cultural realities of man, human communities, peoples and nations, I say to you: with all the means at your disposal, watch over this fundamental sovereignty that every nation possesses by virtue of its own culture. Cherish it like the apple of your eye for the future of the great human family. Protect it! Do not allow this fundamental sovereignty to become the prey of some political or economic interest. Do not allow it to become a victim of totalitarian and imperialistic systems or hegemonies, for which man counts only as an object of domination and not as the subject of his own human existence. For them, too, the nation—their own nation or others—counts only as an object of domination and a bait for various interests, and not as a subject: the subject of sovereignty coming from the true culture which belongs to it as its own. Are there not, on the map of Europe and the world, nations which have a marvelous historic sovereignty derived from their culture, and which are, nevertheless, deprived of their full sovereignty at the same time? Is this not an important point for the future of human culture, important above all in our age, when it is so urgent to eliminate the vestiges of colonialism?

16. This sovereignty which exists and which draws its origin from the specific culture of the nation and society, from the primacy of the family in the work of education, and finally from the personal dignity of every man, must remain the fundamental criterion of the manner of dealing with the problem, an important one for humanity today, namely, that of

the media of social communication (of the information which is bound up with them, and also of what is called "mass culture"). Since these media are "social" media of communication, they cannot be means of domination over others, on the part of agents of political power as well as of financial power which impose their program and their model. They must become the means—and what an important means!—of expression of this society which uses them, and which also ensures their existence. They must take into account the real needs of this society. They must take into account the culture of the nation and its history. They must respect the responsibility of the family in the field of education. They must take into consideration the good of man, his dignity. They cannot be subjected to the criterion of interest, of the sensational and of immediate success but, taking into account ethical requirements, they must serve the construction of a "more human" life.

17. *Genus humanum arte et ratione vivit.* Fundamentally, it is affirmed that man is himself through truth, and becomes more himself through increasingly perfect knowledge of truth. I would like to pay tribute here, ladies and gentlemen, to all the merits of your organization and at the same time to the commitment and to all the efforts of the states and institutions which you represent, in regard to the popularization of instruction at all grades and all levels, as regards the elimination of illiteracy, which signifies the lack of all instruction, even the most elementary, a lack which is painful not only from the point of view of the elementary culture of individuals and environments, but also from the point of view of socio-economic progress. There are distressing indications of delay in

this field, bound up with a distribution of goods that is often radically unequal and unjust; think of the situations in which there exist, alongside a plutocratic oligarchy limited in numbers, multitudes of starving citizens living in want. This delay can be eliminated not by way of bloody struggles for power, but above all, by means of systematic alphabetization through the spread and popularization of instruction. An effort in this direction is necessary if it is then desired to carry out the necessary changes in the socio-economic field. Man, who "is more," thanks also to what he "has," and to what he "possesses," must know how to possess, that is, to order and administer the means he possesses, for his own good and for the common good. For this purpose, instruction is indispensable.

18. The problem of instruction has always been closely linked with the mission of the Church. In the course of the centuries, she founded schools at all levels; she gave birth to the medieval universities in Europe: in Paris and in Bologna, in Salamanca and in Heidelberg, in Krakow and in Louvain. In our age, too, she offers the same contribution wherever her activity in this field is requested and respected. Allow me to claim in this place for Catholic families the right which belongs to all families to educate their children in schools which correspond to their own view of the world, and in particular the strict right of Christian parents not to see their children subjected, in schools, to programs inspired by atheism. That is, indeed, one of the fundamental rights of man and of the family.

19. The system of education is organically connected with the system of the different orientations given to the way of practicing and popularizing science, a purpose which is served by high-level educa-

tional establishments, universities and also, in view of the present development of specialization and scientific methods, specialized institutes. These are institutions of which it would be difficult to speak without deep emotion. They are the work benches at which man's vocation to knowledge, as well as the constitutive link of humanity with truth as the aim of knowledge, become a daily reality, become, in a sense, the daily bread of so many teachers, venerated leaders of science, and around them, of young researchers dedicated to science and its applications, as also of the multitude of students who frequent these centers of science and knowledge.

We find ourselves here, as it were, at the highest rungs of the ladder which man has been climbing, since the beginning, towards knowledge of the reality of the world around him, and towards knowledge of the mysteries of his humanity. This historical process has reached in our age possibilities previously unknown; it has opened to human intelligence horizons hitherto unsuspected. It would be difficult to go into detail here for, on the way to knowledge, the orientations of specializations are as numerous as the development of science is rich.

UNESCO, MEETING POINT OF HUMAN CULTURE

20. Your organization is a place of meeting, a meeting which embraces, in its widest sense, the whole field, so essential, of human culture. This audience is, therefore, the very place to greet all men of science, and to pay tribute particularly to those who are present here and who have obtained for their

work the highest recognition and the most eminent world distinctions. Allow me, consequently, to express also certain wishes which, I do not doubt, will reach the thought and the hearts of the members of this august assembly.

Just as we are edified in scientific work—edified and made deeply happy—by this march of the disinterested knowledge of truth which the scholar serves with the greatest dedication and sometimes at the risk of his health and even his life, we must be equally concerned by everything that is in contradiction with the principles of disinterestedness and objectivity, everything that would make science an instrument to reach aims that have nothing to do with it. Yes, we must be concerned about everything that proposes and presupposes only these non-scientific aims, demanding of men of science that they should put themselves in their service without permitting them to judge and decide, in all independence of mind, the human and ethical honesty of these purposes, or threatening them with bearing the consequences when they refuse to contribute to them.

Do these non-scientific aims of which I am speaking, this problem that I am raising, need proofs or comments? You know what I am referring to; let it suffice to mention the fact that among those who were brought before the international courts, at the end of the last world war, there were also men of science. Ladies and gentlemen, I beg you to forgive me these words, but I would not be faithful to the duties of my office if I did not utter them, not in order to return to the past, but to defend the future of science and human culture; even more, to defend the future of man and the world! I think of Socrates who, in his uncommon integrity was able to sustain that knowledge is at the same time moral virtue, would have to climb down from his certainty if he could consider the experience of our time.

DIRECT SCIENCE TO THE DEFENSE OF MAN'S LIFE

21. We realize it, ladies and gentlemen, the future of man and of the world is threatened, radically threatened, in spite of the intentions, certainly noble ones, of men of learning, men of science. It is threatened because the marvelous results of their researches and their discoveries, especially in the field of the sciences of nature, have been and continue to be exploited—to the detriment of the ethical imperative—for purposes that have nothing to do with the requirements of science, and even for purposes of destruction and death, and that to a degree never known hitherto, causing really unimaginable damage. Whereas science is called to be in the service of man's life, it is too often a fact that it is subjected to purposes that destroy the real dignity of man and of human life. That is the case when scientific research itself is directed towards these purposes or when its results are applied to purposes contrary to the good of mankind. That happens in the field of genetic manipulations and biological experimentations as well as in that of chemical, bacteriological or nuclear armaments.

Two considerations lead me to submit particularly to your reflection the nuclear threat which is weighing upon the world of today and which, if it is not staved off, could lead to the destruction of the fruits of culture, the products of civilization elaborated throughout the centuries by successive generations of men who believed in the primacy of the spirit and who did not spare either their efforts or their fatigue. The first consideration is the following. Geopolitical reasons, economic problems of world dimension, terrible incomprehension, wounded national pride, the materialism of our age and the decadence of moral values have led our world to a situation of instability, to a frail balance which runs the risk of being destroyed any moment as a result of errors of judgment, information or interpretation.

Another consideration is added to this disquieting perspective. Can we be sure, nowadays, that the upsetting of the balance would not lead to war, and to a war that would not hesitate to have recourse to nuclear arms? Up to now it has been said that nuclear arms have constituted a force of dissuasion which has prevented a major war from breaking out, and it is probably true. But we may wonder at the same time if it will always be so. Nuclear arms, of whatever order or magnitude or of whatever type they may be, are being perfected more and more every year, and they are being added to the arsenal of a growing number of countries. How can we be sure that the use of nuclear arms, even for purposes of national defense or in limited conflicts, will not lead to an inevitable escalation, leading to a destruction that mankind can never envisage or accept? But is it not you, men of science and culture, that I must ask not to close your eyes to what a nuclear war can represent for the whole of humanity (cf. *Homily for the World Day of Peace*, January 1, 1980).

22. Ladies and gentlemen, the world will not be able to continue for long along this way. A conviction,

which is at the same time a moral imperative, forces itself upon anyone who has become aware of the situation and the stake, and who is also inspired by the elementary sense of responsibilities that are incumbent on everyone: consciences must be mobilized! The efforts of human consciences must be increased in proportion to the tension between good and evil to which men at the end of the twentieth century are subjected. We must convince ourselves of the priority of ethics over technology, of the primacy of the person over things, of the superiority of spirit over matter (cf. *Redemptor hominis*, no. 16). The cause of man will be served if science forms an alliance with conscience. The man of science will really help humanity if he keeps "the sense of man's transcendence over the world and of God's over man" (*Address to the Pontifical Academy of Sciences*, November 10, 1979, no. 4).

Thus, seizing the opportunity of my presence at the headquarters of UNESCO today, I, a son of humanity and Bishop of Rome, directly address you, men of science, you who are gathered here, you the highest authorities in all fields of modern science. And through you I address your colleagues and friends of all countries and all continents.

I address you in the name of this terrible threat which weighs over mankind, and, at the same time, in the name of the future and the good of humanity all over the world. I beseech you: let us make every effort to establish and respect the primacy of ethics, in all fields of science. Let us do our utmost particularly to preserve the human family from the horrible perspective of nuclear war!

I tackled this subject before the General Assembly of the United Nations Organization, in New

York, on October 2 of last year. I am speaking about it today to you. I appeal to your intelligence and your heart, above passions, ideologies and frontiers. I appeal to all those who, through their political or economic power, would be and are often led to impose on scientists the conditions of their work and its orientation. Above all I appeal to every scientist individually and to the whole international scientific community.

All together you are an enormous power: the power of intelligences and consciences! Show yourselves to be more powerful than the most powerful in our modern world! Make up your mind to give proof of the most noble solidarity with mankind: the solidarity founded on the dignity of the human person. Construct peace, beginning with the foundation: respect for all the rights of man, those which are connected with his material and economic dimension as well as those which are connected with the spiritual and interior dimension of his existence in this world. May wisdom inspire you! May love guide you, this love which will suffocate the growing threat of hatred and destruction! Men of science, commit all your moral authority to save mankind from nuclear destruction.

23. Today I have been given the possibility of realizing one of the deepest desires of my heart. I have been given the possibility of penetrating, here, within the Areopagus which is that of the whole world. I have been given the possibility of saying to all, to you, members of the United Nations Educational, Scientific and Cultural Organization, to you who are working for the good and for the reconciliation of men and peoples through all fields of culture, science and

Today I have been given the possibility of realizing one of the deepest desires of my heart. I have been given the possibility of penetrating, here, within the Areopagus which is that of the whole world. I have been given the possibility of saying to all, to you, members of the United Nations Educational, Scientific and Cultural Organization, to you who are working for the good and for the reconciliation of men and peoples through all fields of culture, science and information, to say to you and to cry to you from the inmost depths of my soul: Yes! The future of man depends on culture! Yes! The peace of the world depends on the primacy of the Spirit! Yes! The peaceful future of mankind depends on love!

information, to say to you and to cry to you from the inmost depths of my soul: Yes! The future of man depends on culture! Yes! The peace of the world depends on the primacy of the Spirit! Yes! The peaceful future of mankind depends on love!

Your personal contribution, ladies and gentlemen, is important, it is vital. It lies in the correct approach to the problems, to the solution of which you dedicate your service.

My final word is the following: Do not stop. Continue. Continue always.

TIME FOR REFLECTION
ON A RICH EXPERIENCE

On Monday afternoon, June 2, the Holy Father left Paris by helicopter for his visit to Lisieux. Before his departure he spoke as follows to the distinguished ecclesiastical and civil authorities who were present at the École Militaire to bid him farewell.

My journey is drawing to its close, as regards the capital. I am very happy at all the contacts through which it has enabled me to benefit. I am beginning to be accustomed to full programs, but I think that, this time, it would not have been possible to do much more! I appreciated the opportunity offered to me to express what my responsibilities dictate to me. I have also "recorded" many testimonies; what I have seen and heard will be for me subject matter for further reflections and above all the object of prayer. It is a rich experience!

It fell to the journalists to report the facts, describe things, and stress the essential, let us say to bear witness in all truth to the event and to emphasize what is really at stake. I hope that is what they have done. That is what honors their duty, of which I have often had occasion to speak. Today, I just wanted to thank them and to thank with them all the agents of social communication, the press, radio and television. In France, owing to their competence and their equipment, their productions are of very high technical quality. They have a demanding public! I offer them all my best wishes, with my deep gratitude.

I must also express my hearty thanks to all members of the police and of the national Gendarmerie, entrusting their representatives here to convey them to their colleagues. You had the task not only of watching over me, but of ensuring order among the innumerable crowds present everywhere, and I am aware of the extra work demanded of you on this occasion. I excuse myself to you and your families.

I was, in fact, and still am, full of admiration for everything that contributed to the service of public order, all along the course of our ways and in places of assembly, and that in spite of the delays in my program, right from the first evening!, which must certainly have complicated the task. You carried it out with remarkable competence and concerted action, with dignity and great devotion. I really thank you heartily! It was your honor to ensure the Pope the best hospitality and to serve the French people at the same time in its desire to take part in these gatherings, for it was certainly the French people that desired it spontaneously.

Without drawing things out, I would like you to know that I appreciate your public service, which is often not sufficiently recognized. A few months ago, I had the opportunity to say so in Rome to a group of French policemen, pilgrims of "Police and humanism." Such are the sentiments I always cherish for your persons and for your duty.

But many other persons must have worked hard
in the last few weeks for this journey, in order to plan
details with French precision. In addition to those of
the Nunciature whom I have already thanked, I am
thinking of the Secretariat of the episcopate and of all
the services that collaborated with this Secretariat to
coordinate the whole thing. I would not like to forget
any of those who dedicated themselves discreetly,
beyond their ordinary work, to cope with the event. I
pray to the Lord to reward all you have done for His
servant and for your brothers, and I willingly bless
your families and those who are dear to you.

To Paris, but not yet to France, I say: "Au revoir!"

FERVENT COMMUNION WITH CHRIST'S SUFFERINGS

Shortly after his arrival at Lisieux, the Holy Father concelebrated Mass in the huge square in front of the Basilica of St. Thérèse of Lisieux. Among the vast congregation present at the Mass were contingents from all over Normandy. After the Gospel the Pope preached the following homily.

1. I am very happy that it has been possible for me to come to Lisieux on the occasion of my visit to the French capital. I am here on pilgrimage with you all, dear brothers and sisters, who have come, you too, from many regions of France, to the one we love so much, "little Thérèse," whose way to holiness is closely linked with the Carmelite convent of Lisieux. If those versed in asceticism and mysticism, and those who love the saints, have acquired the habit of calling this way of Sister Thérèse of the Child Jesus "the little way," it is beyond all doubt that the Spirit of God, who guided her along this way, did so with the same generosity as when He guided her patron, the "great Teresa" of Avila, and as when He guided—and continues to guide—so many other saints in His Church. So glory be to Him for ever!

The Church rejoices in this marvelous richness of spiritual gifts, so splendid and so varied, as are all the works of God in the visible and invisible universe. Each of them reflects man's interior mystery and at the same time meets the needs of the times in the history of the Church and of humanity. This must be said of St. Thérèse of Lisieux who, until recently, was in fact our "contemporary" saint. It is in this way that I see her personally, in the framework of my life. But is she still the "contemporary" saint? Has she not ceased to be so for the generation which is now reaching maturity in the Church? It would be necessary to ask the men of this generation. Allow me, however, to note that saints virtually never grow old, that they never fall under "prescription." They continually remain witnesses of the youth of the Church. They never become characters of the past, men and women of "yesterday." On the contrary: they are always men and women of "the morrow," men of the evangelical future of man and of the Church, witnesses "of the future world."

THE LITTLE WAY OF
HOLY CHILDHOOD

2. "For all who are led by the Spirit of God are sons of God. For you did not receive the spirit of slavery to fall back into fear, but you have received the spirit of sonship. When we cry, 'Abba! Father!'..." (Rom 8:14-15)

It would be difficult perhaps to find words more synthetic, and at the same time more striking, to characterize the special charism of Thérèse Martin, that is, what constituted the quite special gift of her heart, and which became, through her heart a special gift for the Church. A gift marvelous in its simplicity, universal and at the same time unique. Of Thérèse of Lisieux, it can be said with conviction that the Spirit of God permitted her heart to reveal directly, to the men of our time, the fundamental mystery, the reality of the Gospel: the fact of having really received "the spirit of sonship," when we cry, "Abba! Father!" The "little way" is the way of "holy childhood." In this way, there is something unique, the genius of St. Thérèse of Lisieux. At the same time there is the confirmation and renewal of the most fundamental and most universal truth. What truth of the Gospel message is, in fact, more fundamental and more universal than this one: God is our Father and we are His children?

This truth, the most universal one, this reality, was also "reread" anew with the faith, the hope and the love of Thérèse of Lisieux. It was in a way rediscovered with the interior experience of her heart and the form taken by her whole life, which lasted only twenty-four years. When she died here, at the Carmelite convent, a victim of tuberculosis from which she had suffered for a long time, she was almost a child. She has left the memory of the child: of holy childhood. Her whole spirituality confirmed once more the truth of these words of the Apostle: "For you did not receive the spirit of slavery to fall back into fear, but you have received the spirit of sonship...." Yes, Thérèse was the child. She was the child "trustful" to the point of heroism, and consequently "free" to the point of heroism. But it is precisely because it was to the point of heroism, that she alone knew the interior savor and also the interior price of this trust which prevents "falling back into fear"; this trust which, even in the deepest darkness and sufferings of the soul, makes it possible to cry: "Abba! Father!"

Yes, she knew this savor and this price. For anyone who reads attentively her *History of a Soul,* it is clear that this savor of filial trust comes, like the perfume of roses, from the stalk which also bears thorns. If, indeed, we are "children, then we are heirs of God and fellow heirs with Christ, provided we suffer with him in order that we may also be glorified with him" (Rom. 8:17). It is for that reason, precisely, that the filial trust of little Thérèse, St. Thérèse of the Child Jesus but also "of the Holy Face," is so "heroic," because it comes from fervent communion with Christ's sufferings.

When I see before me all these sick and infirm people, I think that they, too, are associated, like Thérèse of Lisieux, with Christ's passion, and that, thanks to their faith in God's love, thanks to their own love, their spiritual offering mysteriously obtains for the Church, for all the other members of the Mystical Body of Christ, a supplement of vigor. Let them never forget this beautiful sentence of St. Thérèse: "In the heart of the Church, my Mother, I will be love." I pray to God to give each of these suffering friends whom I love with very special affection, solace and hope.

THE WHOLE CHURCH
IS MISSIONARY

3. To have trust in God like Thérèse of Lisieux means following the "little way" where the Spirit of

God guides us: He always guides towards the greatness in which the sons and daughters of divine adoption participate. Already as a Child, as a twelve-year-old Child, the Son of God declared that His vocation was to attend to the things of His Father (cf. Lk. 2:49). To be a child, to become like a child, means entering the very center of the greatest mission to which man was called by Christ, a mission that goes through the very heart of man. She knew it perfectly, Thérèse. This mission draws its origin from the eternal love of the Father. The Son of God as a man, in a visible and "historical" way, and the Holy Spirit in an invisible and "charismatic" way, carry it out in the history of humanity.

When, at the moment of leaving the world, Christ said to the Apostles: "Go into all the world and preach the Gospel to the whole creation" (Mk. 16:15), He inserts them, through the power of His paschal mystery, into the great movement of the eternal mission. From the moment when He left them to go to the Father, He begins at the same time to come "again in the power of the Holy Spirit" whom the Father sends in His name. More deeply than all the truths on the Church, this truth has been highlighted in the consciousness of our generation by the Second Vatican Council. Thanks to that, we have all understood far better that the Church is constantly "in a state of mission," and that is what is meant by the fact that the whole Church is missionary. We have also understood better this particular mystery of the heart of little Thérèse of Lisieux, who through her "little way," was called to participate so fully and so fruitfully in the highest mission. It is precisely this "littleness" that she loved so much, the littleness of the child, which threw wide open to her the greatness of the divine mission of salvation, which is the constant mission of the Church.

Here, in her Carmelite convent, in the enclosure of the convent of Lisieux, Thérèse felt specially united with all the missions and missionaries of the Church in the whole world. She felt she was a "missionary" herself, present through the special power and grace of the Spirit of love in all missionary posts, close to all missionaries, men and women, in the world. She has been proclaimed by the Church the patron saint of the missions, like St. Francis Xavier, who traveled tirelessly in the Far East: yes, she, little Thérèse of Lisieux, shut up in the Carmelite cloister, apparently detached from the world. And, thanks to her, Lisieux has become the point of departure of efforts for the external, and also for the internal missions in France.

I am glad to be able to come here shortly after my visit to the African continent, and, in the presence of this admirable "missionary," to give back to the Father of eternal truth and love all that is already the fruit in the power of the Son and the Holy Spirit, of the missionary work of the Church among the men and peoples of the black continent. I would like at the same time, if I may express myself in this way, to borrow from Thérèse of Lisieux the perspicacious look of her faith, her simplicity, and her trust, in a word the youthful "littleness" of her heart, to proclaim before the whole Church how plentiful is the harvest, and to ask like her, the Master of the harvest to send, with even greater generosity, workers to His harvest (cf. Mt. 9:37-38). May He send them in spite of all the obstacles and all the difficulties He meets with in man's heart, in man's history.

THANKS FOR ST. THÉRÈSE

In Africa, I often thought: what faith, what spiritual energy these missionaries of the last century or the first half of this century, had, and all these missionary institutes that were founded, to set off without hesitation to these countries, then unknown, with the one purpose of making the Gospel known, of enabling the Church to be born! They rightly saw in it a work indispensable for salvation. But for their audacity, but for their holiness, the local Churches whose centenary we have just celebrated, and which are now guided mainly by African bishops, would never have existed. Dear brothers and sisters, let us not lose this enthusiasm!

I know, indeed, that you do not wish to resign yourselves to losing it. I greet among you the former missionary bishops, witnesses of the zeal of which I was speaking. France has still a great many missionaries all over the world, priests, men and women religious and laity, and certain institutes have opened themselves to the missions. I see here the members of the chapter of the Foreign Missions of Paris, and I recall the blessed Théophane Vénard whose martyrdom in the Far East was a light and a call for Thérèse. I am also thinking of all the French priests who dedicate at least some years to service of the young Churches, in the framework of *Fidei donum*. Today we understand better, moreover, the necessity of brotherly exchange among the young and the old Churches, to the benefit of both. I know, for example, that the Pontifical Mission Aid Societies, in liaison with the Episcopal Commission of the Missions Abroad, are aiming not only at obtaining the material aid, but at forming the missionary spirit of Christians in France, and I rejoice at this.

I would like..., if I may express myself in this way, to borrrow from Therese of Lisieux the perspicacious look of her faith, her simplicity, and her trust, in a word the youthful "littleness" of her heart, to proclaim before the whole Church how plentiful is the harvest, and to ask, like her, the Master of the harvest to send, with even greater generosity, workers to His harvest (cf. Mt. 9:37-38). May He send them in spite of all the obstacles and all the difficulties He meets with in man's heart, in man's history.

This missionary enthusiasm can arise and bear fruit only on the basis of greater spiritual vitality, of the radiation of holiness.

BROTHERLY EXCHANGE

4. "The beautiful exists in order that it may enchant us for work," wrote Cyprian Norwid, one of the greatest poets and thinkers that Poland has given, and whom France received, and preserved in the cemetery of Montmorency.

Let us give thanks to the Father, the Son and the Holy Spirit for the saints. Let us give thanks for Saint Thérèse of Lisieux. Let us give thanks for the deep, simple and pure beauty which was manifested in her to the Church and to the world. This beauty enchants. And Thérèse of Lisieux has a particular gift to enchant through the beauty of her soul. Even if we all know that this beauty was difficult and that it grew in suffering, it does not cease to delight the eyes of our souls with its special charm.

It enchants, therefore, this beauty, this flower of holiness which has grown on this soil; and its charm constantly stimulates our hearts to work: "The beautiful exists in order that it may enchant us for work." For the most important work, in which man learns thoroughly the mystery of his humanity. He discovers in himself what it means to have received "the spirit of sonship," radically different from "the spirit of slavery," and he begins to cry with all his being: "Abba! Father!" (cf. Rom. 8:15)

Through the fruits of this magnificent interior work the Church is constructed, the kingdom of God on earth, in its deepest and most fundamental substance. And the cry "Abba! Father!" which rings out far and wide in all the continents of our planet, also returns as an echo to the silent Carmelite cloister at Lisieux, vivifying ever anew the memory of little Thérèse, who through her life, short and hidden but so rich, uttered with particular forcefulness "Abba! Father!" Thanks to her, the entire Church has found again the whole simplicity and freshness of this cry, which has its origin and its source in the heart of Christ Himself.

FOLLY TO THE WORLD, WISDOM IN THE SPIRIT

After the Mass in Lisieux on June 2, the Holy Father then visited the Carmel of Lisieux and gave the following address to the contemplative sisters there.

My dear sisters,

1. Peace and joy in Christ Jesus! To you who surround the humble Successor of the apostle Peter! And, through you, to all enclosed nuns in France.

I must tell you first of all of my deep emotion at being able to pray near the shrine that contains the remains of St. Thérèse. I have already expressed at length my thanksgiving and my attachment for the "spiritual way" that she adopted and offered to the whole Church. I now feel great joy at visiting this Carmelite convent which was the setting of her life and her death, of her sanctification, in the midst of her sisters, and which must remain an important place of prayer and sanctification for the Carmelites and for all pilgrims. It is from here that I would like to strengthen you all, whatever your spiritual family may be, in your contemplative life, which is absolutely vital for the Church and for mankind.

YOUR CHALLENGE

2. While loving our age deeply, it has to be recognized that modern thought easily confines to subjectivism everything that concerns religion, the faith of believers, religious sentiments. And this view does not spare monastic life. To such·an extent that public opinion, and alas! sometimes some Christians who tend to appreciate only practical commitment, are tempted to consider your contemplative life as an escape from real life, an anachronistic and even useless activity. This incomprehension may make you suffer, and even humiliate you. I will tell you like Christ: "Fear not, little flock" (Lk. 12:32). In any case a certain monastic revival, which is manifested throughout your country, must buoy up your hope.

But I also add: take up the challenge of the modern world and of the world of always, by living more radically than ever the very mystery of your quite original state, which is folly in the eyes of the world and wisdom in the Holy Spirit: exclusive love of the Lord and of all your human brothers in Him. Do not seek to justify yourselves! All love, provided it is authentic, pure and disinterested, bears in itself its own justification. To love gratuitously is an inalienable right of the person, even—and one should say, above all—when the Beloved is God Himself. In the footsteps of contemplatives and mystics of all times, continue to bear witness with power and humility to the transcendent dimension of the human person, created in the likeness of God and called to a life of intimacy with Him. St. Augustine, at the end of meditations made as much with his heart as with his penetrating intelligence, assures us that man's bliss lies there: in loving contemplation of God! That is why the quality of your belonging lovingly to the Lord, on the personal plane as well as on the community plane, is of extreme importance. The fullness and radiation of your lives "hidden in God" must challenge the men and women of today, must question the young who are so often looking for the meaning of life. Meeting you or seeing you, every visitor, guest or retreatant in your monasteries should be able to say or at least feel that he has met God, that he has experienced a revelation of the Mystery of God who is light and love! The times in which we live need witnesses as much as apologists! Be, on your part, these very humble and always transparent witnesses!

SPIRITUALLY FAITHFUL

3. Let me assure you further—in the name of the constant Tradition of the Church—that not only can your life proclaim God's absoluteness, but that it possesses a marvelous and mysterious power of spiritual fruitfulness (cf. *Perfectae caritatis,* no. 7). Why? Because your loving oblation is integrated by Christ Himself in His work of universal Redemption, in much the same way as the waves merge in the depths of the ocean. Seeing you, I think of the Mother of Christ. I think of the holy women of the Gospel, standing at the foot of the Lord's cross and communing in His salvific death, but also messengers of His resurrection. You have chosen to live, or rather Christ has chosen you to live His paschal mystery with Him through time and space. All that you are, all that you do every day, whether it is the Office intoned or sung, the Celebration of the Eucharist, work in your cells or

in fraternal teams, respect of enclosure and silence, mortifications chosen or imposed by the rule, everything is assumed, sanctified, used by Christ for the redemption of the world. In order that you may have no doubt on this matter, the Church—in Christ's own name—took possession one day of all your powers of living and loving. It was your monastic profession. Renew it often! Following the example of the saints, dedicate yourselves, sacrifice yourselves more and more, without even seeking to know how God uses your collaboration. Whereas at the basis of every action, there is a purpose and therefore a limitation, a finitude, the gratuitousness of your love is at the origin of contemplative fruitfulness. A very modern comparison comes into my mind: you kindle in the world the fire of revealed truth and love, in rather the same way as the masters of the atom light space rockets: from a distance.

THOUGHTS TO ENCOURAGE

4. Finally I would like to add two encouraging thoughts which seem to me opportune. The first concerns faithfulness to the charism of your founders or foundresses. The brotherhood and cooperation that exist more than before among monasteries must not lead to a certain leveling of contemplative institutes. Let every spiritual family watch over its particular identity in view of the good of the whole Church. What is done in one place is not necessarily to be imitated elsewhere.

My second encouragement is the following. In a civilization that is more and more mobile, sonorous and vocal, areas of silence and rest become a vital necessity. Monasteries—in their original style—have, therefore, more than ever the vocation of remaining places of peace and interiority. Do not let pressure from within or without strike at your traditions and your means of meditation. Endeavor rather to educate your guests and your retreatants to the virtue of silence. You certainly know that I had occasion to recall to participants in the plenary session of the Congregation for Religious, on last March 7, strict observance of monastic enclosure. I recalled in this connection the very strong words of my Predecessor, Paul VI: ''Enclosure does not isolate contemplative souls from the communion of the Mystical Body. Far more, it puts them at the heart of the Church.'' Love your separation from the world, perfectly comparable to the biblical wilderness. Paradoxically, this wilderness is not emptiness. It is there that the Lord speaks to your heart and closely associates you in His work of salvation.

These are the convictions that I was anxious to confide to you very simply, my dear sisters. You will make the best use of them, I am convinced. You pray a great deal for the fruitfulness of my ministry. Receive my hearty thanks! Rest assured that the Pope also reaches and very often, in heart and in prayer, the monasteries of France and of the whole world. I hope and I ask the Lord, through the intercession of the holy Carmelite of Lisieux, that strong and numerous vocations will come to increase and renew your various contemplative communities. I bless you from the bottom of my heart, in the name of the Father and of the Son and of the Holy Spirit.

RELIGIOUS LIFE,
A MANIFESTATION
OF CHRIST

After his address to the Carmelites in Lisieux, the Holy Father then met, in the monastery, the leaders of the Union of Major Superiors of France and the members of the permanent committee for religious. He spoke to them as follows.

The talks I had the privilege of having, on Saturday in Paris, with sisters engaged in tasks of evangelization, and just now in this Carmelite convent, with a large group of contemplatives, were intended by me for all monks and all enclosed nuns, for all men and women religious in France, who spend their lives consecrated to Christ in the ecclesial service of prayer or of the apostolate.

To you, dear brothers and sisters, who have been chosen to bear the responsibility for your institutes, I wish to address a special and important encouragement.

The Council has very happily recalled that all authority in the Church is a service and must be lived in the very spirit of the Lord Jesus (cf. Lk. 22:27). This evangelical and imperative norm must not lead you to renounce your own responsibilities. The formula "everyone responsible" which has met with great success for a good ten years now, is valid in a certain sense only. You are seriously responsible in the last resort for the religious spirit of your subjects, their apostolic output, the faithfulness of your institutes to their specific ideal and the quality of their testimony in the Church and the world of today.

I know on the other hand all the work of research and experiments that your congregations have carried out since the Council. The balance sheet includes happy orientations. Take good care that religious life is an "epiphany" of Christ. The modern world needs signs. A starless night is a source of anguish. In a word, see to it that it is accepted everywhere in your religious families that the time has come for the serene and persevering observance of the revised and approved constitutions. Dear brothers and sisters, I trust in your wisdom and courage. I invoke the most abundant blessings of the Lord on yourselves and on your institutes.

GIFT OF STRONGER COMMUNION IN THE SERVICE OF THE GOSPEL

On Monday evening, June 2, John Paul II left Lisieux by helicopter for the Saint Gratien Airport of Deauville. Before boarding the "Air France" plane that would bring him back to Rome, the Holy Father gave the following brief address to the French Prime Minister, M. Raymond Barre, and to the other authorities who were present to bid him farewell.

Mr. Prime Minister,

The time has now come to leave France, at the end of a visit which will remain unforgettable for me, from every point of view. I do not know what memory will be the most outstanding. Every ceremony, every meeting had its own character and was pregnant with intensity, in smaller circles as in the warmth of the crowds. Perhaps it is finally the feeling of having been able to reach the soul of France and of the French people that I will take away with me as a particularly precious boon.

It was a quite exceptional welcome, worthy of the hospitality of France. I wish here, once again, to express my gratitude to the men and women of this country; to families, workers, the young; to all without any exception, and I do so with all my heart. I thank especially the civil authorities who so kindly collaborated in the implementation of the program, and in the first place His Excellency, the President of the Republic, and the whole of the government, and the Municipal Council of Paris and that of Lisieux.

To my brothers and sons of the Catholic Church, bishops, priests, men and women religious, laity, I leave, on bidding them farewell, the gift that has been bestowed on us of a stronger communion, in the service of our mission of proclaiming the Gospel. We are going to resume this mission with new energy, in proportion to the vastness of the task. God be praised for permitting us to bear witness to Him in this way!

Farewell, dear people of France, or rather *au revoir*. I offer you my most fervent wishes and I bless you in the Lord's name.

To my brothers and sons of the Catholic Church, bishops, priests, men and women religious, laity, I leave, on bidding them farewell, the gift that has been bestowed on us of a stronger communion, in the service of our mission of proclaiming the Gospel. We are going to resume this mission with new energy, in proportion to the vastness of the task. God be praised for permitting us to bear witness to Him in this way!

Farewell, dear people of France, or rather *au revoir.* I offer you my most fervent wishes and I bless you in the Lord's name.

IN THE SERVICE
OF FAITH
AND HUMAN VALUES

On Monday, June 2, at 10:12 p.m., the Holy Father landed at Fiumicino Airport, where he was met by the Minister for Education, Adolfo Sarti, representing the Italian government; numerous cardinals; members of the Diplomatic Corps and other religious and civil authorities.

1. My hearty thanks, Mr. Minister Adolfo Sarti, for the kind expressions of greeting and homage that you have addressed to me, on behalf of the Italian government, as I set foot again on the soil of Italy. At the end of this apostolic journey, which took me beyond the Alps to the noble and beloved French nation, which has acquired in the course of the centuries, innumerable merits with regard to the Church and history, among the many feelings that well up in my heart, I feel mainly that I have to express my most sincere thanks.

To God, in the first place, for the gift He granted me of carrying out this desired pilgrimage, in a spirit of obedience to that mandate of strengthening the brothers, which the Lord Jesus Christ has entrusted to me, calling me to the supreme responsibility as Pastor of the universal Church, in Peter's See.

2. I thank further His Excellency, President Giscard d'Estaing, and the other French political, civil and military authorities, and, in particular, my venerated brothers in the episcopate for their affectionate welcome: together with them I express my gratitude to all the priests, men and women religious, seminarians, workers and Catholic associations, to which I had the pleasure of addressing my word of exhortation. I still think of all those faithful who in Paris and Lisieux gave me such spontaneous demonstrations of devotion and affection, and, what is more important, of deep and sincere participation in the liturgical celebrations of the divine Word and of the Eucharist.

It is not possible at this moment to sum up, even briefly, the most significant moments that I had the possibility of living in Paris, in the great metropolis with its ancient Christian traditions, and at Lisieux, the admired city of St. Thérèse of the Child Jesus, the little and great saint, who does not cease to speak of God to the hearts of the men and women of our time, so thirsty for spiritual values. It was an extremely consoling meeting with the People of God in France, who responded with a great act of faith to the Pope's visit.

3. I also had the opportunity to visit the headquarters of UNESCO, to greet the qualified representatives of the various nations and to open my heart to them on the varied and vast themes concerning the commitment for ever more adequate cultural promotion, dwelling particularly on the Christian meaning of culture itself. I am sincerely grateful to the Director General, Mr. Amadou Mahtar-M'Bow, and to all the personalities I met there, for their cordial welcome.

The service of the Church and of man expands more and more and demands that the Pope be present wherever the requirements of faith and the affirmation of true human values call him. It is to strengthen this Christian faith and to promote these values that the Pope sets out along the ways of the world.

And now, returning to my Roman See, I am particularly happy to greet the Lord Cardinals and the other ecclesiastical personalities present here; and while I renew the expression of my gratitude to Mr. Minister, I extend my respectful greeting to all the Italian political, civil and military authorities, to the representatives of the city administration of Rome, as well as to the members of the Diplomatic Corps and all those who have come to give me a cordial welcome on my return.

May the Lord reward you for such courtesy and shower choice heavenly graces upon you.

GRATITUDE

At the general audience on Wednesday, June 4, the Holy Father began his address with the following introduction about his recent journey to France.

1. Today I wish to express my gratitude to God for the grace of the service which I recently had the privilege of carrying out in Paris and Lisieux.

Invited by the Director General of UNESCO, I had the opportunity to address the 109th session of the Executive Council on last June 2, and to speak of the importance and tasks of culture in the life of man, of the nations and of humanity. At the same time, the Archbishop of Paris did his utmost in order that my presence might become a real pilgrimage and a real pastoral service not only for the Church in Paris but, indirectly, for the whole of France. I thank the episcopal conference, headed by its president, for this. I also thank the President of the French Republic, the representatives of the district for their benevolent attitude to my visit; and, as regards the stay in Paris, I thank the mayor of that stupendous capital.

I am grateful to the Bishop of Bayeux and Lisieux for the invitation to the shrine of St. Thérèse of the Child Jesus; I am grateful likewise to the community and the authorities for the hospitality extended to me. In this way my pilgrimage was able to have full missionary eloquence at the tomb of her whom the Church has declared patron saint of the missions.

Let these first words of thanks, which I address at the same time to all those to whom I owe real gratitude for the preparation and course of the visit, suffice for today. It would be difficult, however, not to seek a fuller form to manifest the importance of this event. I intend to do so on a forthcoming occasion.

THE WHOLE CHURCH
IS MISSIONARY

During the general audience in St. Peter's Square on Wednesday afternoon, June 11, the Holy Father delivered the following address.

1. I return constantly in thought to the recent visit to France: to Paris and Lisieux—and today I wish to make known, at least partly, what it was for me.

In the first place, it was an invitation, which came through men, but it would be difficult not to see in it the finger of Providence. This visit was not foreseen. Some time ago I had considered the journey to the International Eucharistic Congress at Lourdes, which will take place in July, 1981. On the other hand, the invitation to Paris emerged only recently, in relation to a special event, the UNESCO session.

Here I wish to thank particularly Mr. Amadou Mahtar-M'Bow, the Director General of that world organization, who, already some time ago, had invited me to visit it.

The initials UNESCO mean: United Nations Educational, Scientific and Cultural Organization. We are, therefore, in the sphere of the great structure of the United Nations, which, since the end of the terrible Second World War, has become a special need of our age. In spite of the many difficulties of which we are all conscious, it does not cease to serve the cause of the peaceful coexistence of the nations of the whole earth. In October of last year I had the honor to take part in the plenary meeting of the United Nations Organization in New York, following upon the invitation from the Secretary General, Dr. Kurt Waldheim. Subsequently, in November of last year, on the invitation of the Director General, Mr. Edouard Saouma, I was a guest at the Rome headquarters of FAO, the United Nations Organization for Food and Agriculture, which deals, in the global dimension, with problems linked more fundamentally with man's life. We are utterly convinced of this, we who, according to Christ's own words, constantly ask the Father: "Give us this day our daily bread." Through these words we feel what a problem hunger, lack of bread, is for modern men, particularly in some areas of the earth....

MOTIVATION FOR THE VISIT
TO UNESCO

2. In the same dimension of the whole of humanity, at the international level, UNESCO serves the cause of culture, science and education. These are the problems in the sphere of which man lives and develops as a man, as a person, and as a community, as a family, as a nation. Indeed "man shall not live by bread alone" (cf. Mt. 4:4)...or rather, the problems of bread are connected with the level of culture, science and ethics. UNESCO is not directly in the service of the problem of bread, but of questions of culture, education and science—and, therefore, of the problem within which there is manifested and confirmed more deeply what man is, precisely as man. Therefore the

organization which dedicates all its activity directly to these problems has a quite essential importance for the consolidation in the world of the rights of man, of the family, of a nation, for the assurance of human dignity by means of the correct relationship with truth and with freedom.

All these problems, so near to the tasks of the Church in all times, and especially in our age, constituted an ample motivation for my visit to the headquarters of UNESCO on June 2. It created a special occasion to highlight that relationship of the Church with culture, which found its expression in the teaching of the Second Vatican Council, and particularly in the Constitution *Gaudium et spes*. This visit was also the occasion to recall, by means of a special appeal to scientists of the whole world, the great cause of peace.

THE POPE'S GRATITUDE

3. Paris remains the city particularly suited to act as host to the headquarters of UNESCO. Thanks to the initiative of the Archbishop of Paris, Cardinal Marty, the visit to the headquarters of that organization had at the same time a fully pastoral character in regard to the Church in France. I speak of it with special gratitude, which I address both to the representatives of the Church and to those of the citizens and the individual civil authorities.

Together with the French episcopate, I greatly appreciated the significant participation of the President of the French Republic, his words of greeting, as well as the participation of the whole government, headed by the Prime Minister, and of the diplomatic corps.

As regards the city of Paris, it would be difficult not to express gratitude to the mayor and the city council, as well as to all the citizens. I must say the same with regard to the visit to Lisieux.

Allow me to extend these expressions of gratitude to all the persons and institutions that contributed to the organization of this visit, and ensured its course. I am thinking particularly of those to whom I was not able to express this gratitude personally—and towards whom I feel such a debt of obligation. I thank them for having made possible for me, at all the stages and in every detail, the service for which I had come to France. Thank you for having done so with such delicacy, understanding, benevolence, with such mastery and cordial hospitality.

THE CHURCH IN FRANCE

4. The pastoral service of the Bishop of Rome concerns the Church particularly, but it concerns at the same time society, all men, the "world" in which this Church is present—and to which she is sent. In the course of these few days I had the privilege of participating, particularly, in the mission that the Church is carrying out in Paris, and thus, indirectly, I was able to participate in the mission that she is carrying out in the whole of France. A particular expression of this participation was the meeting with the whole conference of the French episcopate under the guidance of Cardinal Roger Etchegaray and with the participation of the other cardinals, all the archbishops and bishops of France. The collegial view of the rich and not easy perspective of the tasks connected with the episcopal mission with regard to one's own social environ-

ment, must be completed with a broader view, if for no other reason than the influence that the French Church, as well as French culture, exercise beyond the frontiers of that nation.

It is a Church that has great merits both as regards the emergence of forms of consciousness and of Christian spirituality, and for the carrying out of missionary activity. The visit to Lisieux, therefore, seemed very justified in order to honor St. Thérèse, who from the Carmelite convent of that city indicated to many contemporaries a special interior way to God—and whom at the same time the Church has recognized as the patron saint of missions in the whole world.

The awareness that the whole Church is "missionary," that she is always and everywhere *in statu missionis*—an awareness to which the Second Vatican Council gave such full expression—seems to offer new impetus particularly to Catholicism in Paris and in France. It would be difficult to analyze here, on the one hand, the particular motives that contribute to that and, on the other hand, the various forms of action of this Church, which bear witness to it.

In the course of my brief visit I had the privilege of meeting the priests, seminarians, the sisters of both active and contemplative congregations, the various groups of the lay apostolate, the International Catholic Organizations, the Catholic Institute in Paris, the world of labor at St. Denis, and the young.

UNFORGETTABLE MEMORIES

They are unforgettable memories. Particularly the last two "open" meetings, with the participation of some tens of thousands of persons, carried out—as regards the meeting with the young—with the method of "dialogue," have remained deeply impressed in my heart. It cannot be forgotten that Paris and France have given hospitality, for some generations, to many Polish emigrants, whom I was able to meet during the visit—as well as other groups, particularly the Portuguese and Spanish, which have increased considerably in recent times. To that must be added the meeting—which, in a way, continues to last—with the inhabitants of Paris first of all, and then of Lisieux, in the large squares, along the streets, and especially along the Seine, from the first evening. This meeting had also its "program," though not communicated, and its eloquence.

I remember with gratitude all the places in which I had the privilege of celebrating the Eucharist—in particular, in front of the Cathedral of Notre-Dame, before the Basilica of St. Denis, where the kings of France rest, at Bourget, in front of the Basilica of Lisieux, and the places where I was able to pray together with the inhabitants and with those who had come from outside: in particular in Rue du Bac and Montmartre.

I keep in my memory the ecumenical meeting, full of deep content and—I think—of mutual understanding; as also the meeting with the representatives of the Jewish religious communities—and with the representatives of the Muslim communities, which are rather numerous at present (nearly two million). I also keep in my memory the various meetings with men of science and culture, with writers and artists. All the meetings are part of a whole that is very varied and complex, with a program that was perhaps too crowded, but very rich and authentic, for which I thank God and men incessantly.

"Do you love?" "Do you love me?" Christ asked Peter after the resurrection. I repeated the same question in the homily in front of the main entrance to Notre-Dame, showing its key significance for the future of man and the world, of France and the Church. I hope that in this question we were able together to find again Him who is the cornerstone of history and—together with the eldest daughter of the Church—become aware of how deeply we come from Him, and of how intensely we must fix our eyes on Him, Christ, on these ways that lead us—as Church and as mankind—to the future.

INDEX

Daughters of St. Paul

IN MASSACHUSETTS
    50 St. Paul's Ave. Jamaica Plain, Boston, MA 02130;
      617-522-8911; 617-522-0875;
    172 Tremont Street, Boston, MA 02111; 617-426-5464;
      617-426-4230
IN NEW YORK
    78 Fort Place, Staten Island, NY 10301; 212-447-5071
    59 East 43rd Street, New York, NY 10017; 212-986-7580
    7 State Street, New York, NY 10004; 212-447-5071
    625 East 187th Street, Bronx, NY 10458; 212-584-0440
    525 Main Street, Buffalo, NY 14203; 716-847-6044
IN NEW JERSEY
    Hudson Mall — Route 440 and Communipaw Ave.,
      Jersey City, NJ 07304; 201-433-7740
IN CONNECTICUT
    202 Fairfield Ave., Bridgeport, CT 06604; 203-335-9913
IN OHIO
    2105 Ontario St. (at Prospect Ave.), Cleveland, OH 44115; 216-621-9427
    25 E. Eighth Street, Cincinnati, OH 45202; 513-721-4838
IN PENNSYLVANIA
    1719 Chestnut Street, Philadelphia, PA 19103; 215-568-2638
IN FLORIDA
    2700 Biscayne Blvd., Miami, FL 33137; 305-573-1618
IN LOUISIANA
    4403 Veterans Memorial Blvd., Metairie, LA 70002; 504-887-7631;
      504-887-0113
    1800 South Acadian Thruway, P.O. Box 2028, Baton Rouge, LA 70821
      504-343-4057; 504-343-3814
IN MISSOURI
    1001 Pine Street (at North 10th), St. Louis, MO 63101; 314-621-0346;
      314-231-1034
IN ILLINOIS
    172 North Michigan Ave., Chicago, IL 60601; 312-346-4228
IN TEXAS
    114 Main Plaza, San Antonio, TX 78205; 512-224-8101
IN CALIFORNIA
    1570 Fifth Avenue, San Diego, CA 92101; 714-232-1442
    46 Geary Street, San Francisco, CA 94108; 415-781-5180
IN HAWAII
    1143 Bishop Street, Honolulu, HI 96813; 808-521-2731
IN ALASKA
    750 West 5th Avenue, Anchorage AK 99501; 907-272-8183
IN CANADA
    3022 Dufferin Street, Toronto 395, Ontario, Canada
IN ENGLAND
    57, Kensington Church Street, London W. 8, England
IN AUSTRALIA
    58 Abbotsford Rd., Homebush, N.S.W., Sydney 2140, Australia